The Author's experience was primarily technical. Obviously, Mathematics was absolutely necessary. He was influenced by Pythagoras who insisted that 1+2+3+4=10, is the perfect number. This is the base of our money and measurement system. Pythagoras is well known by his theorem. In a right angled triangle, the square of the hypotenuse is equal to the sum of the squares of the other two sides. Although Pythagoras discovered this theorem it existed long before Pythagoras was born. It is this a priori – assumptions about human nature; it has made progress in distinguishing the difference between man and beast. Metaphysics and ethics cannot be neglected.

To Maureen, my dear wife, whose constructive criticism and endless encouragement made this publication possible, and a big thank you to Janice Bruford for her valuable assistance.

Maurice Webb

KNOWLEDGE, POWER, WEALTH AND WISDOM

AUSTIN MACAULEY PUBLISHERS™

LONDON * CAMBRIDGE * NEW YORK * SHARJAH

A CIP catalogue record for this title is available from the British Library.

ISBN 9781035802593 (Paperback)
ISBN 9781035802609 (ePub e-book)

www.austinmacauley.com

First Published 2023
Austin Macauley Publishers Ltd®
1 Canada Square
Canary Wharf
London
E14 5AA

KNOWLEDGE devoid of virtue is mere vanity; POWER devoid of values is sure calamity; WEALTH cannot be invested in immortality; WISDOM originates from the ultimate reality.

Table of Contents

Preface   11

Chapter 1: World of Wonder   13

Chapter 2: Narration of Knowledge   30

Chapter 3: Logic and Language   48

Chapter 4: God and Godlessness   64

Chapter 5: Ethics and Egoism   85

Chapter 6: State and Society   102

Chapter 7: Economics and Extravagance   125

Chapter 8: Education and Etiquette   149

Chapter 9: Homes and Health   162

Chapter 10: Environment and Energy   173

Chapter 11: Philos Sophia   182

Bibliography   193

Abbreviations   197

Preface

During his life, the author has accumulated many debts, not concerning money but debts of gratitude. Most of the sums owed are to persons who have departed from the physical world and some have made great contributions to our cultural and social systems.

To avoid infringement of copyright law, permission has been obtained to quote from the commendable *Classics of Western Philosophy* edited by Steven M Cahn and published by the Hackett Publishing Company, Inc. Acknowledgement must be made for the information received from **HM** Treasury and the Balance of Payments figures extracted from the Blue Books of the Office for National Statistics.

In addition, the quotations from the unique two volumes, *The Open Society and Its Enemies* are by kind permission of the estate of Sir Karl Popper; also, acknowledgement must be made for permission to quote from *The Affluent Society* by John Kenneth Galbraith and published by Andre Deutsch Ltd. Finally, the author is indebted to the late Dr Anthony Chadwick whose lectures on the 'Philosophy of Religion' were pleasant stimuli.

In seeking wisdom, thou art wise;
in supposing thou hast acquired it,
thou art foolish.

– Rabbi Ben Azai

Chapter 1
World of Wonder

Aristotle proclaimed, 'It was through wonder that men now and at first began to philosophise.' All intelligent human beings and maybe less intelligent human beings have wondered how our world came into existence. The planet Earth on which we live is one of eight planets of the solar system which is an oblate spheroid in form and its axis is deviated by a strange angle of 23 ½ degrees from the true vertical to the ecliptic. One rotation of its own axis in a period of 24 hours is equivalent to one day and a calendar year is the total time it takes to revolve one elliptical orbit round the sun; the complete process leading to the wonder relating to the phenomenon of the four seasons.

Wonder compels us to choose from two hypotheses:

(i)   is our world partly or wholly related to the mathematical genius of a creator? or

(ii)   is it the result of a cosmic accident, a big bang, from which complex systems have evolved from lava chaos? The planet Earth is influenced by the satellite known as the Moon which revolves around the Earth, whereby the oceans rise and fall twice each day, caused by the gravitational pull of the Moon. Our planet Earth is surrounded by a mixture of gases, the nearest areas often affected by water vapour. The crust of the Earth contains fossil fuels and minerals and in the 'atomic theory of matter,' the compound substances can be divided into molecules.

Our planet Earth is host to flora, fauna and human beings. All human beings are endowed with a brain; an organic device of exquisite sensitivity, which separates and identifies the various flavours in food and drink via the sense of taste; that identifies pleasant or obnoxious odours via the olfactory sense; that hears and identifies sounds of harmony or discord via the aural sense; that observes and identifies objects via the optic sense; and also identifies the qualities of objects when touched via the sense of feeling. Via the five perceptive senses plus intuition, the brain, which is the nerve centre of mental activity, needs constant exercise to stimulate the process of thought for the acquisition of a high level of intelligence.

In western philosophy, the first recognised scholar was a Greek named **Thales** who was born prior to 600 BC in Miletus. He was mainly concerned with the question, 'What is the *stuff* out of which all things originate?' The answer submitted by him pointed to water as the original *stuff* and as such, a substratum, he was prompted to conclude that the Earth floats on water. Possibly, he was drawn to this conclusion after his observation of water in its three forms-liquid, solid and vapour, and due to temperature variation could exist as water, ice or steam.

The next scholar to issue his theory was **Anaximander** who also belonged to the Milesian school. He rejected the theory put forth by **Thales** contending that the world consists of qualitative oppositions that separate from the 'infinite.' There is a balance between the qualities hot and cold, wet and dry. Fire will melt snow and water will extinguish fire. **Anaximander** conceived the origin of matter to be a mass in a state of perpetual motion, whereby slowly, the separate qualities started separating from the 'infinite' as well as each other. Of course, criticism of this theory centres on the viewpoint that quality and substance are considered as the same *stuff*.

A third scholar of the Milesian school, **Anaximenes** said that not water, but air although invisible included everything, so it was the original *stuff* out of which everything issued. Air is the breath of life which he identified with the soul and he affirmed this infinite substance is the *stuff* supporting life. **Anaximenes** completes the triad of Milesian philosophers whose views we now know to be untenable; they were called physiologies and their hypotheses stimulated the spirit of enquiry.

Undoubtedly, **Pythagoras** is the philosopher most known by his theorem linked with the sides of a right-angled triangle. **Pythagoras** was really an enigma who was preoccupied with both mysticism and mathematics. He formed a religious brotherhood that believed in the transmigration of souls and the eating of animal flesh was forbidden since when eating a bird or beast, it may happen to contain the soul of your grandmother.

Pythagoras made an investigation into the musical scales and in these numerical tone and half-tone progressions, he discovered information that enhanced his belief about the whole structure of the world. Numbers in the form of ratios were directly related to the musical scales. The concordant intervals of the different musical scales involved these ratios; first, the octave is 1:2; the fourth is 4:3; the fifth is 3:2. **Pythagoras** equated the universe with *cosmos* which implicates the notions of order, fitness and beauty; the sum of 1+2+3+4=10 is a perfect symbol of the harmonic relations of the world. Of course, discord equates to the uncanonical.

Pythagoras asserted that 'Numbers introduce mathematics' which is a proposition that tends to defy modern logic, yet their numerical structure in the nature of musical sound means we cannot entirely dismiss his proposition. He claimed that all harmony is dependent upon the relation of numbers; that certain numbers such as zero, 1 and 4, frequently occur in so many eventualities that true knowledge is acquired by the use of numbers, and denied the accepted maxim at the time, 'like is known by like.'

Just as we refer to 'the Twelve' meaning the Apostles, the 'evil seven' meaning the seven deadly sins, so the Pythagoreans likewise referred to 'the Two' as a compound of two substances. The origin of all numbers is the God that constructed them who was called the 'One' or 'Unity' because it is the source of all the numbers. From the 'One' is derived the limited and unlimited numbers in opposition. The 'One' remains at a higher level and combines both in a moral and aesthetic order. In this structure of the moral order, the limited represents what is good; conversely, the unlimited represents what is evil. Of course, the limited and the unlimited is meaningful to existing society, especially in the concept of unlimited freedom.

Pythagoras was the originator of a habit developed by many philosophers succeeding him, namely, the habit of marrying all their religious and moral ideas with valid reasoning. All of the earliest philosophers thought that change occurred in a natural way. They observed water changed to ice, air change to wind, and numbers changed to things, everything involved motion. The problem of permanence and change emerged; it appeared that everything changes, yet permanence indicated that there can be no change. Here was the first metaphysical question to arise.

Heraclitus asserted, 'The world is an ever-living fire kindled in measures and in measures going out.' For him, fire was the original *stuff,* and everything is in a state of flux. Moreover, everything was in a state of strife, and he blamed Homer for his love of peace, since rest and motionless existed only among the dead. **Heraclitus** did not identify the universe with a creative deity and regarded God as only a mortal man and man a mortal God.

It was **Parmenides's** destiny to raise a metaphysical argument based on the logic of words. He asked, 'Can the word 'become' have any real meaning?' Can a thing be changed? To change means 'to become what it is not,' or if it came into being, it is not, which is obviously untrue. The principal doctrine presented by **Parmenides** is that Being alone relates to truth and that non-Being relates to nothing. Although the argument was invalid, it was difficult to dispute at that time. Whereas **Heraclitus** argued that everything changes, **Parmenides** counter-argued that there is no change, 'Being is, non-Being is not;' what is permanent can never change. More than 2,000 years later, this problem was resurrected in the form of 'existentialism.'

Parmenides was responsible in a meritorious way for hustling philosophers away from the world of appearances to the world of reality. **Empedocles** agreed with **Parmenides** in his belief of unchangeable being in contrast to the coming into being which he thought impossible. He admitted the existence of plurality and the material world in which there are two forces, strife and love. Strife, by whose nature causes each element to separate from each other, and yet every particle is inclined to mix with others of the same element. Love, by whose nature causes the mingling of elements to create a higher level of being. Thus, there is just separating and mingling of elements and no change takes place.

Pythagoras stated, the most perfect number is the number of numbers in the series and when added together the result is the number 10, which now exists as the base of the decimal as well as the metric system. Empedocles postulated that the universe is a composite sphere of four elements or 'roots,' earth, water, air and fire which are the only realities. Also, each element is composed of millions of small particles which could be mixed in various proportions to produce the multitude of things existing in the universe. The religious side of **Empedocles** is revealed when he suggested that love is the key to the relationship between the sexes and which causes men to consider others prompting them to act morally. Contrarily, strife causes men to harm others and to do evil.

Anaxagoras pointed to the motion of matter and the motion of mind(nous) claiming that there must be a moving cause that is not related to matter. Mind has the power to shape the world and has created order out of a chaotic state. It must not be forgotten that the Greeks never referred to a Genesis whereby a God created something out of nothing, The Greeks believed the concept of creation was the planning and arrangement of order, *cosmos,* within a universe where matter existed as a form of lawless disorder.

Anaxagoras paved the way for the acceptance of a mind that imposed certain conditions and circumstances upon the universe which introduced valid reasoning into the religious argument. Ironically, **Anaxagoras** was persecuted by the state for having a tendency towards atheism for the law permitted charges to be made against any citizen who showed anti-religious behaviour by not speculating about 'the things on high.' Before passing on, it is apt to mention that the dictum of **Anaxagoras**, 'mind rules the world' was acknowledged by the Sophists.

The conception of the universe as a mass of elements involved in mingling, separating and rotating motion made a big impact upon the **Atomists.** Their doctrine denied the reality of the coming into Being, both of the 'Many out of the one' and of the 'One into Many,' claiming that Being is no more than non-Being. Being is the full extended corporeal and non-Being is the void.

The conclusion deduced from their propositions is that Being relates to a thing and non-Being relates to nothing. The notion of the void having existence was accepted by **Pythagoras** when we recall his conviction that zero is a real number. Hence, the **Atomists** believed that everything consists of an infinite number of very small invisible particles acting and reacting in continual motion within the boundless void. These atoms devoid of any qualities differ in only size and shape yet remain invisible.

In claiming that atoms are the *stuff* of the universe, it showed the **Atomists** to be hardened materialists, who believed the soul consists of atoms and the *nous* of **Anaxagoras** was really only a physical process. They countered the powerful argument of **Parmenides** by introducing the existence of the void which then negated the claim that motion was impossible. It was **Aristotle** who criticised the **Atomists** for failing to address the question, 'What is the origin of motion?' The consideration of final cause or purpose was absent in the deliberations of the **Atomists**.

Regarded by many as the greatest western philosopher, **Plato** had been impressed by **Pythagoras** so much, he came to the conclusion that mathematics possessed the key to unlock the secrets of the universe. The academy where he used to teach had this inscription over the entrance, 'Let no one enter here who has not learnt mathematics.' **Plato** contended that pure mathematics is not derived from perception; it is nothing more than a tautology analogous to 'wonders are wonders,' although inclined to be more complex. Mathematics has a peculiarity as it involves only the meaning of symbols and not words.

Plato's 'World of Wonder' consists of two worlds; there is the sensible world or the world in which our perceptive senses all operate, but it is a copy world, not the real world. He argued that objects of knowledge exist only as perfect originals in an ideal world or the world in which ideas abound. The distinction between sense perception and intellectual activity has deeply penetrated the domain of philosophical thought known in the trade as **Plato's** 'Theory of Ideas.'

Ideas were never brought into being by their internal nature for they have forever existed. The piece of furniture, the table we see to place things upon is a copy of the idea of a table, that caused the designer of the table to have it produced. Of course, over a period of time, the table will suffer from neglect or may become damaged, and eventually it will be destroyed. However, the concept or the original idea of the table cannot be destroyed; it belongs to the ideal world which alone can give us knowledge of 'universals.'

Aristotle tried to answer the question, 'How can inanimate matter be linked with permanent eternal forms?' His answer emerged in two related ideas:

(i)   in the idea of immanent form and
(ii)   in the idea of potentiality.

He came to the conclusion that form and matter are inextricably linked; so, they are not *transcendent,* only *immanent* in nature; they exist always in some physical body. Further, he made use of Plato's answer to **Parmenides**, 'It is.' The verb 'to be' entails two very different meanings:

(i)   to exist and
(ii)   to be related to a certain predicate.

Aristotle conceived the dual idea of 'being' as either potential or actual.

In this 'World of Wonder,' let us return to Genesis to consider the apple tree. Let us accept, a seed unifying form and matter grew into an apple tree. As the seed germinated and grew, it was naturally inclined to develop the form of an apple tree. The seed that germinated in the soil was a small portion of matter intent on achieving the form of the apple tree. After maturity, the apple tree produces fruit in the form of the apple and in the core of the apple exists the seed which has the same form as the original seed although it is different matter. In all instances, the seed, the apple tree and the apple, there exists form and matter. Matter can be changed but never destroyed whereas form can never be changed; form is eternal.

Plato believed that God created the universe by introducing eternal forms, but according to **Aristotle,** the universe has existed always, so there was no beginning. God was not a creator but a cause, the cause of all causes. God is the cause of all motion in the universe yet God remains motionless and self-inspired. The complex of nature is guided by a final cause which is identified with God and the universe is a process of self-creation. The God of Aristotle is a static, perfect, eternal God who is the first cause on which all the causes of motion and change in the universe ultimately depend for their existence. From such premises, we arrive at the conclusion of **Aristotle**, that is, God is really the 'unmoved mover.'

Aristotle's conclusion may not be appreciated by some as his God conveys the impression of a cold, causal God in isolation, so any relationship appears to lack a formal cause. He taught that matter and form must be studied, 'Further, matter is relative to something: for each form has a different matter.'

Aristotle listed four kinds of causes:

(i)   material cause
(ii)   formal cause;
(iii)   efficient cause;
(iv)   final cause.

'A block of marble is a latent statue' and the sculptor is dependent upon the marble. So, the material cause of the statue is the marble; the formal cause is the form to be realised; the efficient cause, 'the source of the primary origin of the change;' in other words, the operation of the chisel on the marble; and the final cause is the purpose or end that the sculptor had in mind.

About 300 BC, a pupil of **Plato** produced one of the specialist achievements of the Hellenistic Period. **Euclid** established the basis of all geometrical theory in his 'Elements of Geometry.' During this period, two main schools emerged and both became preoccupied with the question, 'How to live a good life?' The concept of 'good' is related to the world in which the good life is pursued. So, both the **Epicureans** and the **Stoics** contrived to find answers appertaining to the nature of the universe. The **Epicureans** were materialists who mainly accepted the theory of the **Atomists**. The universe came into being by mere chance, for atoms do not always follow a straight path for when falling down in space, they tend to swerve. The **Stoics** did not follow the **Epicureans** who refused to believe in chance and taught that the role of nature was determined by natural laws. They were impressed by the view of **Aristotle**, namely, that the universe is composed of two entities—form, (force) and matter. Force is that which tends to move and matter is acted upon.

Pyrrho was the founder of the school of Sceptics who said that nobody knows, and nobody ever can know. Any attempt to discover the nature of things was abandoned and the nature of the universe was beyond human understanding. Every question receives the same answer, 'Perhaps' or 'Maybe;' there is a firm refusal to express an opinion. This philosophy is a form of dogmatism denying the possibility of any knowledge about the nature of the universe or the stewardship of planet Earth.

During the third century, Plato's doctrines were resurrected and the new doctrines became known as **Neoplatonism.** Due to the unstable and chaotic state of matter, **Plato** considered that matter is evil. Therefore, the Neoplatonists thought that all the conflict in the world resulted from the separation of matter from its 'ideal form.' They believed that a mystical union with the 'One' was achieved by isolating the individual soul from the material world. Neoplatonism emerged as a direct challenge to Christianity, extracting major parts from Greek philosophy. The trinity of **Plotinus** comprised the Platonic Good, the 'One' of **Aristotle** and the Stoic system of ethics.

Augustine was another Neoplatonist who was convinced that God created matter from non-existent matter. This enabled God to plan and to structure prior to creating the universe. The distinction between the **Greek** philosophers and **Augustine** is significant; whereas he believed that the forms resided in God's mind which came into being after the creation of matter from nothing, the Greeks assumed that matter and forms have **always** existed.

In his unique book called *Confessions*, **Augustine** made this statement, 'You, O God almighty…You are the Maker of all time and before all time. What then is time?…Neither past nor future can he time, since the past is no more and the future is not yet. On the other hand, if the present were always present and never flowed away into the past, it would not be time at all, but eternity. The present is a moment…and we measure time in its passing…we are aware of periods of time; we compare one period with another…While time is passing it can be measured; when it has passed it cannot, for it is not.' It is difficult to explain the passing of time, for either time itself flows or human beings move in time. Time differs from space as it has only one dimension and its course is irreversible.

Before the Middle Ages, the desire of the Christian society to become a church had been fulfilled, but the desire of the Church to rationalise its dogmas as well as its constitution remained unfulfilled. The philosophers who undertook this task were given the name, *scholastici* which means school teachers; hence, this became known as the period of 'Scholasticism.' This period of thought was associated with the ideas of **Aristotle** and attempted to justify Christian beliefs. The 'World of Wonder' became the 'World of Theology.'

Thomas Aquinas, the famous Doctor of Theology, reduced the chasm between theology and philosophy by maintaining that the existence of God can be confirmed from the direct proofs of reason. Therefore, reason and philosophy alone were used to support the doctrines of the church which had suffered from extreme criticism. In his *Summa Theologia,* **Aquinas** listed five arguments relating to God's existence, and as he was a realist, he believed that all universals existed in the mind of God. He agreed with the other schoolmen that God created the universe without the existence of matter, which is united with universals in the system of nature. **Thomas Aquinas** conceived creation as a continuous activity.

The controversy about universals is related to the one-many or one-over-many problems which was highlighted by **Plato** who treated universals as objects separate from their forms. **Aristotle** maintained that there is no separation from their forms as they exist as real things. The viewpoints are associated with realism, which identifies universals as follows:

(i)   universals prior to the object(s) or

(ii)   universals in their object(s).

In the Middle Ages, **William of Ockham** regarded universals as signs which had arisen naturally, therefore, *nominalism* means that individual objects can be recognised, but any conclusions about them are mere ideas in the mind. *Conceptualism* accepts that universals are dependent upon mind but shared by many minds. The authors of the Bible and **Aristotle** claimed that the Earth was the centre of the universe, whereby Heaven was a place containing all the stars and angels; Hell or the Inferno was the centre of the Earth where the devil dwelt. Design and purpose revealed a divine hand and everything moved in a circle. It has been suggested that 'History is a record of phases,' but also, it is a record of sin and crime when reflecting upon the initiation of the Crusades. There were eight military expeditions arranged under the ensign of the Cross with the Papacy leading the cause to regain the Holy Land occupied by the Saracens. The centuries of theological conflict prompted some men to turn to mathematics and science and this development can be traced back to the fifteenth century. **Nicolas Copernicus,** a Polish astronomer, declared that previous thinkers had erred in their method of explaining the motion of the planets but agreed that their motion was circular. He contended, 'In this most beautiful temple, could we place this 'Great Light' in any better position from which to illuminate the whole at once? In the middle of all sits the Sun, enthroned, ruling all the planets which circle around this 'Royal Throne'.

Later, a German astronomer, **Johannes Kepler** postulated the view that orbits of planets were not circular but elliptical. **Kepler** propounded an important law, namely: the time taken for a planet to orbit the Sun relates to its distance from the Sun; the square of the time of the elliptical revolution is proportional to the planet's mean distance from the Sun. He also discovered that tides are caused by the gravitational pull of the Moon.

In the year 1590, **Galileo** set about a significant experiment that made a great impact on the subject of Physics. From the famous 'Leaning Tower of Pisa,' he simultaneously dropped two weights-a 1 lb weight and a 100lbs weight from a point 100ft above ground level. The observers of **Galileo's** experiment were convinced that the heavier weight would fall faster than the lighter weight. They believed the 100lbs weight would fall 100 feet while the 1 lb weight was falling through one foot. To their surprise, the observers witnessed the two weights hit the ground almost the same instant.

The result of **Galileo's** experiment as well as those of similar experiments carried out by **Isaac Newton,** guided the latter to express the gravitational pull of the Earth in mathematical terms. By applying **Kepler's** 'Law of Planetary Motion,' **Newton** was drawn to the conclusion—the force of gravity is inversely proportional to the square of the distance of the object. Whatever the size, whatever the shape of the object provided that the effect of wind resistance is ignored, the acceleration is the same. **Newton** formulated three 'Laws of Motion' although the third law is also important in the 'Design of Structures,' that is, 'To every action there is an equal and opposite reaction.'

These scientific discoveries caused disarray in the church or the 'City of God' for many of its basic beliefs were shown to be false. It was believed that the Earth was a flat plateau with the dome of Heaven above. The discoveries dictated that the whole geography of Heaven and Hell had to be abandoned. The places were imaginary so the places became conditions. The Catholic church remained sceptical about the discoveries for more than two centuries before it accepted the facts. However, the church recovered from its predicament by discovering that scientists could not prove 'there is no God,' since attempting to prove a negative is virtually impossible.

Francis Bacon claimed that scientific progress depended on devising a new method, namely induction, to solve the problems of science. He maintained that no real scientific advance would be possible until men had broken away from the 'authority' of **Plato** and **Aristotle** as well as the mediaeval 'schoolmen,' so science must become value-free for it to function properly. True! The application of science in the production of dreadful weapons was not the fault of science; but if a scientist wishes to remain value-free, then what is the difference between the computer and such a scientist? Such a question was precluded by **Bacon** when he claimed that 'man can act and understand no further than he has observed.'

Known as the father of Modern Philosophy, **Rene Descartes** believed that substance is the *sub/rate* of all that exists in the universe. He claimed that God is the absolute substance and two other substances, mind and matter, exist independently of each other. God created these two substances separating them into two different worlds, the material world and the mental world. Descartes conceived the material world as mechanical, so forms, ideas and universals were eliminated from his machine-like world, and God supplied a certain definite generator of motion that cannot be destroyed. Mind is isolated from this mechanical world and its activity includes thinking, believing, understanding, doubting, reasoning and inferring.

For **Descartes,** the nature of mind and body were completely incompatible. He asserted that there is 'one chief property of substance that constitutes its nature and essence: that is, *extension* makes up the physical nature of substance, and thought makes up the mental nature of substance.' This dualism means that the motion of the hammer's arm is unrelated to the striker's mind. So, **Descartes's** Theory avoids the interrelation of events in the mental world with the physical world. Ironically, his theory unwittingly introduced another problem; determinism versus free-will, as Cartesian philosophy eliminated free-will because physical laws are firmly deterministic. **Benedict Spinoza** thought that mind and matter were related to thought and extension. They were two attributes of one as well as the same substance called God. His theory of 'psychophysical parallelism' states that mind and matter are independent because the one universal substance is God or Nature, so there exists thought and action subject to motion in parallel lines. **Spinoza** attempted to eliminate the dualism of **Descartes** by recognising the pantheistic nature of the world. The power behind the universe and within everything in the universe is God.

Leibniz disagreed with **Descartes's** Theory by denying that extension can be an attribute of substance because extension includes many and must involve a sum-total of substances for each single substance has no extension. **Leibniz** asserted that substance is composed of many centres of force or *monads,* and they are 'the very atoms of nature.' However, they are not atoms of matter for as each monad is a soul, they are spiritual entities. In his essay called 'The Monadology,' he wrote, 'Bodies act as if there were no souls and souls act as if there were no bodies, yet both act as if each influenced the other.'

Descartes, Spinoza and **Leibniz** have been labelled as the 'Continental Rationalists' who appealed to reason only in their arguments. **Locke, Berkely** and **Hume** have been labelled as the 'British Empiricists' who all appealed to sense-experience in their arguments. **John Locke** claimed that our senses give us information about the 'World of Wonder.' The sense organs are the means to gain experience and they are the first steps in gaining knowledge. **Locke's** position on universals is clearly in the court of *Nominalism* and he asserted that the general idea of 'man' when it may involve many of the same class is nothing more than a name.

The philosophy of **George Berkely** can be reduced to an epitome, *'esse est percipi'* meaning, 'to be is to be perceived.' He was certain that the universe existed only in the minds of human beings together with the mind of God. This philosophy has been called 'subjective idealism' although Berkely referred to it as 'immaterialism.' This absurd conclusion emerges; if no actor is on the stage, then the stage as well as the scenery are non-existent.

Berkely claimed, things are only the ideas we have of them. **David Hume** agreed partly with **Berkely**, but considered that the 'science of man' as the only thing known in the universe. All we can know to exist is that which is within our own minds, all other minds do not exist, and all objects are just ideas in our minds. **Hume**'s opinion that only minds and mental events exist can only admit *solipsism* derived from the Latin *solus* and *ipse,* translating, 'self-alone.' **Hume**'s philosophy can be seen to be a criterion of doubt, whereas **Berkely**'s philosophy was a criterion of faith.

In the beginning of the fifth section of his 'Enquiry Concerning Human Understanding,' **Hume** wrote:

'All the objects of human reason or enquiry may naturally be split into two kinds, to wit, *Relations of Ideas* and *Matters of Fact. That* the square of the hypotenuse is equal to the sum of the square of the two sides, is a proposition which expresses a relation with these figures…Propositions of this kind are discoverable by the mere operation of thought, without dependence on what is anywhere existent in the universe…Matters of fact which are second objects of human reason, are not ascertained in the same manner…All reasonings concerning matter of fact seem to be founded on the relation of *Cause* and *Effect.'*

Hume provided the idea for an effective scientific method; it involves more than the observation of just one instance of any 'cause and effect' relationship. **Hume**'s concept has been superseded by *probability Theory* which is the mathematical theory shadowing probability arguments and most induction processes.

Immanuel Kant is alleged to have said that **Hume**'s ideas on causality awakened him from his dogmatic slumbers. He affirmed that the universe causes only the act of sensation, but our minds apprehend this act in space and time by providing the concepts underlying our experience. **Kant** made this assertion: the 'thing-in-itself' or the *noumenon,* which is the cause of our sensation, does not exist in space and time, so cannot be known. The Rationalists produced their thesis, thereby prompting the Empiricists to produce the antithesis, then **Kant** produced the synthesis. So, **Kant**, like **Plato**, proclaimed the existence of two worlds. **Jean Jacques Rousseau** came to be accepted as the father of the Romantic Movement, whereby a sensibility emerged that demanded involvement of the emotions rather than the sole use of reason. In his 'Discourse on Inequality,' he claimed that 'man is naturally good,' and it is only the social system that made him bad. In many respects, natural inequality is inevitable, but he disliked the inequality that privileges permit. **Rousseau** had no time for the science culture as it had the tendency to enslave man by attempting to eliminate the human factor. He rebelled against the dehumanisation of man to the level of being of an inanimate machine, and crusaded for man's return to nature as a 'noble savage.'

A hundred years between the middle of the eighteenth century and the nineteenth century reveal the significant progress made in science. By experimenting with frogs, **Luiga Galvani** was able to show how the contraction of the muscle generated an electric current. Later, **Alessandro Volta** generated an electric current with acid of dissimilar metals isolated by pads in salt water. **Andre Ampere** discovered that a wire in which flows an electric current generates a magnetic field at right angles to its own plane. Then, **Michael Faraday** reversed the process whereby a magnetic field is able to 'induce' an electric current in a conductor. By introducing a rotating magnet so as to produce a continuous electric current, he paved the way for the emergence of the dynamo for large power generation.

At the beginning of the nineteenth century, a Quaker from Cumberland published his radical 'New System of Chemical Philosophy' in which he outlined his atomic theory of matter. He discovered that air contains a mixture of gases whose densities varied, yet the heaviest gas declined to descend to the bottom of the mixture. He concluded that the gases forming the mixture of air separated into minute particles, which accounted for air not inclined to split into 'layers' of oxygen, carbon dioxide and nitrogen. **John Dalton** proposed the atomic theory of atoms.

Avogadro, an Italian physicist claimed that atomic groups which make up compound substances can be sub-divided into molecules. This led to the formulation of **Avogadro's** Law: that equal volumes of different gases at the same temperature and pressure contain each the same number of molecules. **Hegel** embarked upon a 'voyage of discovery' when working on his book called

Phenomenology of Mind as the 'thing-in-itself' of **Kant** transcended both reason and logic, **Hegel's** active 'Absolute Idea' involved the unity of reason and logic. From the proposition, 'the Absolute is Pure Being,' we are led to the antithesis resulting from the insistence that pure being without any qualities is nothing, therefore, the 'Absolute is Nothing.' The synthesis is born from the union of Being and non-Being, and the result is Becoming which is stated as 'The Absolute is Becoming.'

This three-fold method is used to show that knowledge starts with being conscious of an object through our sensory perception, followed by doubt about the reliability of our senses, until the desire for self-knowledge becomes almost irresistible. **Hegel** was influenced by **Socrates** in agreeing that man's highest form of knowledge is self-knowledge. He maintained that for the Absolute, there is nothing external to it to know as the Absolute is the Whole. The total reality is spirit whereby pure thought leads to human thinking about pure thought. This is how God has intervened in human affairs throughout history. **Hegel's** philosophy is known as *objective idealism*.

August Comte established what he called the 'Positive Philosophy' which involved the belief that the scientific spirit had evolved via three stages—The Theological Stage or The Mythical Stage, The Philosophical or Abstract Stage, and finally, the Scientific Stage or Positive Stage. However, via a secret entrance, he admitted a fresh religion called the Religion of Humanity which interested other faiths long before **Comte** was born. He thought that knowledge was only acquired by observation and experience. Know-how and behaviour study were the central topics of 'Positivism.' The meaning and purpose of anything cannot be obtained because the possibility of objective knowledge was disclaimed. This closed-circuit philosophy denying the existence of metaphysics was nothing more than a life-denying type of metaphysics. The core of metaphysics is 'Ontology' which is the study of 'Being' or all that exists, and involves the question—does anything exist necessarily?

In 1843, *A System of Logic* by **John Stuart Mill** which was a method that could be used by social science as well as the natural sciences. **Mill's** definition of induction is:

the process by which we conclude that what is true of certain individuals of a class is true of the whole class, or what is true at certain times will be true in similar circumstances at all times.

The canons of induction have been reduced to a simpler method of progress: change one part or factor at a time; observe and study the result.

Using the information provided by the two mathematicians, **George Boole** and **Gottlob Frege,** who both maintained that mathematics was reducible to logic, **Bertrand Russell** and **Alfred North Whitehead** produced their bible of logic called *Principia Mathematica.* They explained that mathematics is a more comprehensive expression of the propositions of logic. The syllogism which had been held in high esteem was reduced to a small part of the predicate calculus.

Einstein produced his thesis, 'General Theory of Relativity' which challenged the independent concepts of space and time as conceived by **Newton.** **Einstein** insisted that the separation of space and time was an error; the time factor should be replaced by a four-dimensional continuum of space-time. The significant part in the theory is that absolute velocity cannot be measured since speed must always be relative to the observer.

Following the new theory about space and time, it produced a new relation between the mass of a body and its amount of energy. **Einstein** constructed his famous formula: $E = mc^2$. By increasing the energy in the particle, we increase the mass of the particle.

Max Planck developed his hypothesis which showed that in a minute particle of matter, namely, the atom, there existed a minute portion of energy and he expressed it as a *quantum* of energy. The 'Quantum Theory' reveals that in the sub-atomic world, events are unpredictable. Action takes place in this world without cause. Electrons have neither a specific motion nor an exact location; the only thing certain about their nature is their uncertainty. This unpredictable predicament was expounded by **Heisenberg** in his 'Principle of Uncertainty.'

In 'The Mysterious Universe,' **James Jeans** made reference to **Plato** 's simile of the cave in drawing attention to many scientists' view of the universe.

All the pictures which science now draws of Nature are pictures of mathematics. When scientists study the world of phenomena, the shadows which Nature throws on the wall of our cave, they do not find these shadows totally unintelligible, and neither do they seem to represent unknown or unfamiliar objects…Nature seems very conversant with the rules of pure mathematics, just as our mathematicians have formulated them in their studies, out of their own inner consciousness and without drawing to any appreciable extent on their experience of the outer world.

We have considered with disfavour the possibility of the universe having been planned by a biologist or an engineer; from the intrinsic evidence of the creation, the Great Architect of the universe now begins to appear as a pure mathematician.

In writing *Philosophy and the Physicist*, **Susan Stebbing** focused on the fundamental error made prior to the *quantum* laws. The Principle of Uncertainty eliminates any reason there may have been for regarding the material universe as a huge machine. The machine-picture has never been worked out in detail but the ideal of a machine has been imaginatively grasped by physicists and, in consequence, language appropriate to machine behaviour has been extensively used.

The persistence of human beings to identify themselves with rational animals and the universe as a massive machine tended to spread the gospel of atheism. It appears to be poetic justice now that some scientists admit that the 'Big Bang' theory was merely an explosion of human hot air, The Anthropic Principle appears to have resurrected the belief in a divine being, as it is now acknowledged that the balance of forces in the universe, from the sub-atomic to celestial bodies is so perfect, the odds against the universe being partly planned for human beings by way of an accident were 10^n where n is an index subject to variation. Reason and faith are similar to body and mind, they are interrelated.

Chapter 2
Narration of Knowledge

Reflecting upon the above title, it seems absurd to condense the mountainous store of knowledge into one chapter; however, in justifying this action, it must be emphasised that the most significant parts of substantial knowledge will be highlighted, especially the greatest study. When a person makes an error or perhaps a false judgement, then it shows a lack of knowledge. It appears paradoxical for an author to state in his foreword that his book may possibly contain errors prior to making his assertions. Is it consistent to declare, 'I believe some of my beliefs are false?'

In **Plato's** *The Hepubhc,* Book VI, Adeimantus admonished **Socrates**, (paraphrased as follows):

"Do you think that anyone is going to let you now escape without asking you what this greatest study is, which is something beyond justice.

Socrates responded: The Idea of the Good is the supreme object of all knowledge, and it is by their relation to it that just actions as well as all the objects of desire become useful and beneficial. Although our knowledge of it is limited, yet if we lack knowledge of it, even comprehensive knowledge of other things **will be** useless. Suppose we possess the whole world, is there any gain for without the Good nothing else has real value?

Many believe that pleasure is the only Good, whereas an *intelligent* person believe it is knowledge. However, when the *intelligent* are asked— 'Knowledge of what?' They are compelled to answer:

'Knowledge of the Good.'

Socrates continued: Of course, it is. They blame us for not knowing what the Good is and then pretend they know what it is. Those who define the Good as pleasure appear just as confused. Do they say the same things are both good and bad. We all seek the Good, yet it cannot be adequately comprehended what it is. It does not have the firm understanding about it as other things.

Adeimantus taunted **Socrates**: This Idea of the Good; you have told us what the opinion of others is, but you have failed to give us your opinion.

Socrates responded: My friend; I am only able to tell you about what resembles a satellite of the supreme Good. We speak of the many beautiful things and good things, and we say these many things are the objects of sight, known by the perceptive sense but not by thought. As you know, the eyes are the sense of sight and the objects seen may have colours present, but without a third kind of thing, the function of the other two things is impaired.

Adeimantus inquired: What is this third kind of thing?

Socrates replied: LIGHT; the other two things are dependent upon it. Which of the Gods in the heaven can you hold responsible for this, whose light allows us to see so many beautiful things?

Adeimantus retorted: Obviously, the SUN.

Socrates continued: The relation of the sun to sight in the visible world is like the relation of the GOOD to the intelligence in the mental world. So, it is also a mistake to think knowledge and truth as Good-like; it is wrong to think of either as the Good, for the Good must be honoured more than truth or knowledge. You must think of the good dominating the world of ideas just like the sun dominates the world of visible things. It is like a line divided into two unequal parts, one represents the visible world, the other the intelligible world. The two parts are then divided in the same ratio."

Wisdom	'*Understanding*, dialectical thinking concerned with the ideas of justice, temperance and fortitude relating to truth, beauty and goodness.'
	_____
KNOWLEDGE relating to the things which are unseen in the mental world	Reasoning, mathematical thinking concerned with triangles, squares, symbols etc. and kindred sciences
	_____
	Perception, concerned solely with visible things and uncritical opinion

OPINION   ———

Imagination, concerned with the
images of things and vagueness.

Ignorance

The divided line shows the four parts of knowledge appertaining to the visible world and the mental world. In the visible world are the images of things, the living creatures around us, all plants and the whole class of manufactured things. The intelligible world is divided in such a way, so that in geometry, axioms are constructed from which certain conclusions are drawn.

Understand also, in contrast with this type of thinking, there is the dialectical method of thinking. It does not consider its hypotheses as first principles, but more as hypotheses in the true sense of stepping stones and starting points. Hence, we reach that which is beyond hypothesis, without making use of anything visible, namely, the first principle of reality which is the sovereign GOOD.

Plato was dismayed by a group of thinkers who were called the **Sophists** who firmly believed that knowledge relating to the nature of the universe is unattainable. Knowledge belongs to only the first person as one of them. **Gorgias** dogmatised, nothing exists, and if it did, no one could know it, and if they knew it, they could not communicate it.

At that time, this was the type of sceptical opinion which tended to fascinate the business community who paid for the services of these astute men. The **Sophists** were professional consultants engaged in the business of purveying advice to clients concerning the techniques involved in persuasion and rhetoric. Primarily, the information they sold was nothing more than a sales gimmick aided by sophisticated language. These charlatans became proficient in the art of 'making the worst cause seem the better.' The most prominent member of the Sophists, **Protagoras** asserted, 'Man is the measure of all things.' **Socrates** deduced that the advice that these clever fellows offered was inconsistent with their belief. How was it possible for these professional teachers to give advice to their clients and at the same time assert it was impossible for any knowledge whatsoever to be communicated? **Socrates** argued that because the Sophists lacked knowledge, they were unqualified to give instruction, for they had no idea of distinguishing between doing the right thing and the wrong thing.

The artifice of instructing human beings in 'how to get away with it' was contrary to good leadership. The art of leadership involved more than the practice of 'getting away with it.' It demands ethical judgements to show how human beings ought to tread. It is a certain kind of knowledge that is indispensable in any form of society. Ironically, **Protagoras** opened the door to knowledge through which he could not pass. In proclaiming 'Man is the measure of all things,' **Protagoras** failed to identify the qualities which are common to all human beings, and it prompted **Socrates** to assert, 'the proper study of mankind is man.'

In **Plato's** *Symposium,* **Socrates** made a statement which is extraordinary in its simplicity, paraphrased as follows: 'The curse of ignorance is that a man who is neither good nor wise remains self-satisfied; he has no desire to acquire that of which he feels no need.' In employing the word 'ignorance,' **Socrates** signified a lack of wisdom. He questioned, 'How can a man be satisfied if he does not know what he is or why he was born?' A man who is not concerned about these two questions appears to lack an inquiring mind.

The door to happiness is not via the key of self-satisfaction; it is via the key of self-knowledge. **Socrates** received the key from the Delphi oracle who was renowned for her divine guidance offered to those who were perplexed. The key was engraved with the famous two words, **KNOW THYSELF**. The dialogue *P baedrus,* contains this significant statement by **Socrates**, 'I must first know myself as the Delphian inscription says; to be curious about that which is not my concern, while I am still in ignorance of my own behaviour would be ludicrous.'

Muhammad, the founder of the Islamic religion was asked by **Ali**, "What am I to do so that I do not waste my time?" The reply from **Muhammad** was, "Learn to know thyself." In a letter to the Romans, St Paul made his confession:

We know that the law is spiritual but I am a slave to sin. My own behaviour perplexes me and I do not understand what I do. What I wish to do, I do not do, but what I do I hate to do. If I do what I do not wish to do, then I know the law is good. As I am aware of my behaviour, it must be sin that dwells within me.

It is appropriate to quote the observation of **Alexander Pope** paraphrased as follows:

A little knowledge is a dangerous thing;
Drink deep from the perpetual spring.
Shallow draughts intoxicate the brain,
But drinking heavily sobers us again.

Traditional wisdom recognised that self-knowledge must be a priority in an adult education system. Of course, self-analysis, knowing one's mind, was firmly embedded in Oriental religious doctrines long before psychology was established as a science. Ancient psychology was not concerned about human beings who needed to be cleansed of their abnormal behaviour, but insisted upon purifying normal behaviour to a point where psychological analysis was unnecessary. The 'Doctrine of Awakening' stresses that it is to change from thinking about one's self to knowing about one's self. In seeking self-knowledge, the person will be obtaining knowledge that will be of assistance in understanding the internal world of other human beings.

Plato thought that those men who love beautiful objects are persuaded by appearance, whereas those men who love beauty independent of objects have the knowledge of reality. In his *Symposium,* **Diotima** explains to **Socrates** the ascent from the love of physical beauty to the love of beauty itself. There are four profound steps in the ascent from the physical world to the spiritual world and thence to the eternal world. From the low philistine world, the first step is the love of physical beauty. From physical beauty, the next step demands that we must love moral beauty. Moral beauty in the mind, which includes the beauty of moral law and the beauty of justice. To protect moral beauty, the next step demands that we must love rational beauty embracing the beauty of logic.

The final step, beyond physical beauty, moral beauty, and rational beauty, beyond the beauty of all the different kinds of knowledge, such as mathematics and biology, there is the vision of beauty itself, free from physical desire and material dust. **Diotima** informed **Socrates** that a man who completes the ascent will be able to contemplate divine beauty. Then he will be able to bring forth not mere reflected images of goodness, but true goodness. Thus, the human soul will make contact with the ultimate object of love, so a human soul will become immortal in a divine sense.

Aristotle was moved by his biological studies in believing that the universe is *teleological* in Nature. He pointed to the fact that we do not ascribe to chance or mere coincidence the frequency of rain in winter, so he concluded that there is action for an end present in Nature. Hence, Nature has knowledge of design and purpose. For **Aristotle**, true knowledge was attained in knowing the causes and reasons for the phenomena in the world. From this standpoint, he formulated the 'Doctrine of the Four Causes' and 'Laws of Thought' which are embodied in the containing the skeleton structure for deductive reasoning.

Both the Epicureans and the Stoics disagreed with **Plato** who argued that ideas are innate. The two schools claimed that all knowledge is acquired by sense perception, we learn from the exercise of our senses and knowledge is written on the blank tablet that we possess when we enter the world. Both groups of philosophers insisted that we have no knowledge whatsoever at birth until our first sense perception, which originates from the heavy hand of the midwife. The Greek scholars brought forth the two opposite viewpoints which have dominated different thinkers throughout the period of 'Modern Philosophy.' Those who accepted **Plato's** viewpoint are called *rationalists;* those who trust the senses are called *empiricists.*

Rene Descartes, in seeking a basis for certain knowledge returned to **Pythagoras** for inspiration. His conviction that a mathematical language existed in the universe showed him the way to accept something that it was impossible to doubt. In his quest for certain knowledge, **Descartes** noticed that his ideas were neither clear nor distinct; they originated from his hazy experiences of the past or from mists of imagination. Innate ideas are not associated with such experiences or imaginations. The basic entities of mathematics and the concept of pure being, God, are ideas unrelated to experience as they are innate. **Descartes** wrote two books which have had a huge influence upon western philosophy; their titles are *Discourse on Method* and *Meditations.* Both stress the importance of a sceptical attitude as a prelude to obtaining certain knowledge. In the *Meditations*, this extract shows his distrust of the senses:

All that up to the present time I have accepted as true and certain I have learned either from the senses or through the senses; but sometimes, I have learnt that these senses are deceptive, and it is wiser not to trust entirely anything by which we have once been deceived. The problem about the senses was recognised. After postulating on the awful possibility of being deceived by God, **Descartes** wrote:

On the contrary, I judge God to be infinite in act and goodness. Certainly, it entered my mind that God could have given me a nature such that I might be deceived, yet it is contrary to his nature. (However) let him who can deceive me; as long as I think that I am something, he will never bring it about that I am nothing, or one day make it true that I never existed, and then one has no choice but to conclude that from the simple fact that I exist and that an idea of a most perfect being, that is God, is in me, it is most evidently demonstrated that God exists.

Descartes argued that to attempt to prove his dictum was false remained an impossibility, for immediately *I think* the proof emerges. These three famous words, *cogilo ergo sum,* 'I think, therefore I am,' have been labelled **Descartes** *cogito.* It is relevant to repeat a story about an American philosopher, **Morris Raphael Cohen,** who set his students the task of reading **Descartes's** *Meditations* for homework. The following morning a bleary-eyed young man waylaid **Professor Cohen**; he told the professor that he had missed going to bed because he was not certain that he existed. Appealingly, he burst out, "Tell me, **Professor Cohen**, please tell me, do I exist?"

The Professor paused and responded, "Who is asking the question?"
"I am," came the timid reply.

Plato and **Descartes** belong to the rationalist school since they both maintained that reason is the most reliable guide to attain knowledge. **Descartes's** reason led him to accept the dualism of mind and matter that had originated from **Plato**. Mind and matter are considered as two independent spheres allowing attention to be focused on one or the other without association.

It has been suggested that the Dutch philosopher, **Benedict Spinoza,** conjoined Jewish mysticism and Christian concepts in his pantheist theology. He employed the Cartesian Method and the ideas of clarity and distinction in his main work, 'Ethics,' which is based on the system of **Euclid**. Whereas **Descartes** confirmed the existence of three substances, God plus mind and matter, **Spinoza** emphasised the existence of a single substance, namely, *Deus sivenatura,* meaning God or Nature. **Gottried Liebniz,** a German mathematician, completes the triad of Continental Rationalists. He is associated with the statement confirming that Cartesian philosophy is the 'ante-chamber' of truth. The truth was only accessible after a barrier had been removed. Whereas **Spinoza's** philosophy was centred on a single substance and **Descartes** thought there were three substances, **Leibniz** in his 'Theory of Monads,' asserted that there exist an infinite number of substances. He defined a monad as a centre of force, something spiritual, unlike atoms which are particles of matter.

Leibniz insisted that the world of reality is composed of centres of force rather than particles of matter. These centres of force or monads belong to a hierarchy structure, in which some have a higher status due to their clarity and precision, although 'without windows,' in forming a mirror of the universe. This hierarchy of monads begins with simple types fixed in their properties according to nature, and ending with the monad of all monads, in a single word, God.

In his work, 'The Monadology,' **Leibniz** wrote, 'According to my system, bodies act as if there were no souls, and souls act as if there were no bodies, and both act as if each influenced the other.' The reality of matter was unacceptable to **Leibniz** who thought that each monad views the world in private perspective. If a number of things are all members of the same class and all embody common properties, then they are identical in the sense of equating to really only one thing. This principle is known as the *identity of indiscernibles,* and as a monad is literally a group of one, it follows that two monads can be exactly alike.

Leibniz stated that our reasonings are based on two great principles—that of contradiction, in which we judge that which involves a contradiction to be false and that of sufficient reason, whereby we consider that we can find no true or existent fact, no true assertion, without there being a sufficient reason why it is thus and not otherwise, although most of the time, these reasons cannot be known to us. There are two kinds of truths—those of *reasoning* and those of *fact.* The truths of reasoning are necessary and their opposite is impossible; the truths of fact are contingent, and their opposite is possible. When a truth is necessary, its reason can be found by analysis. In his famous 'Essay Concerning Human Understanding,' **John Locke** rejected the rationalist notion claiming the presence of innate ideas, counter-claiming that all our ideas are derived from sense experience. He wrote:

To say a notion is imprinted on the mind, and yet at the same time to say that the mind is in ignorance of it, and never took notice of it, is to make this impression nothing. Let us then suppose the mind to be, as we say, white paper void of all characters, without any ideas…Whence has it all the materials of knowledge and reason? To this, I answer in one word, from EXPERIENCE. In that, all our knowledge is founded; and from that it ultimately derives itself…For to imprint anything on the mind without the mind perceiving it, seems to be hardly intelligible…there is nothing in the intellect which was not previously in the senses. The two great and principal actions of the mind which are most considered are—*Perception* or *Thinking; Volition* or *Willing.*

He postulated that any idea in the mind must relate to the 'quality' of the external object. His idea caused him to separate sensations into two categories, that is, the primary and secondary qualities. The primary qualities are those that are firmly and positively connected to the body or object, and are listed as solidity, size, shape, motion, cessation of motion and number. The secondary qualities are not located in the object itself, but emerge via some power able to produce sensations in us by their primary qualities. The secondary qualities such as colours, sounds, odours, taste and touch reactions are inextricably linked to the efficiency of the human sense organs, and they depend on the primary qualities.

George Berkeley was an Irishman who disagreed with **Locke**. In the first of his 'Three Dialogues,' he argued:

Colours, sounds, tastes, in a word, all those termed secondary qualities, have certainly no existence without the mind but by this acknowledgement I must not be supposed to derogate anything from the reality of matter or external objects, seeing it is no more than several philosophers maintain, who nevertheless are the farthest imaginable from denying matter. For the clearer understanding of this, you must know sensible qualities are divided into *primary* and *secondary.* The primary qualities they hold exist really in bodies. All sensible qualities beside the primary, that they assert, are only ideas existing nowhere but in their mind.

Whereas **Descartes** and **Locke** both accepted that the object of the mind is nothing else but an idea, **Berkeley** insisted that all objects are nothing else but ideas. **Berkeley** denied the existence of matter and argued that there are no independent material objects. We only experience a sequence of ideas, which prepared the ground for the laying down of his famous dictum relating to the existence of things, or quoting in Latin, *esse est percipi*, translating, 'to be is to be perceived.' So, there remains no doubt about **Berkeley's** conclusion— material objects merely exist from the act of being perceived. This dictum summarises **Berkeley's** philosophy which has been labelled, 'subjective idealism,' but **Berkeley** preferred to call it 'immaterialism.'

David Hume completes the trio of the British empiricists. Strange that **Hume** was a radical sceptic and **Berkeley** was a passionate believer, yet they both agreed about the nature of abstract ideas. In his 'Treatise of Human Nature,' he contended that abstract ideas are in themselves individual, however, they may become general in their representation. He asserted that everything we are conscious of results from either impressions or ideas. Impressions are more forceful and active than the ideas, so impress the mind more readily. All our simple ideas in their first appearance are derived from simple impressions; complex ideas need not appear as impressions. Imagination allows us to have a complex idea of an angel without the sense experience of sight, but the composition of this complex idea originates from an impression. The transition from simple ideas to complex ideas has no rational association as the association is related to the imagination.

Hume was convinced that we do not perceive a relation which is *causal* in comparing the association of ideas with the principle of universal attraction in physics he wrote. 'Here is a kind of attraction which in the mental world will be found to have as extraordinary effects as in the natural world, and to show itself in as many and as various forms. Its effects are everywhere conspicuous; and must be resolved into original qualities of nature, which I pretend not to explain.' **Hume** was certain that no 'force' or 'necessity' can be perceived to reveal the existence of any causal connection. **Hume's** philosophy of scepticism made him a stranger to both religion and science.

Immanuel Kant, a German philosopher, synthesised the 'Continental Rationalists' and 'British Empiricists' branches of philosophy. He achieved this unity of opposition by initially producing a critique of our faculties. **Hume's** denial of cause prompted him to declare, 'The cause and effect relation exists only in our imagination; there is no law confirming that cause precedes effect.' **Kant** refused to accept **Hume's** statement that this law could not be verified.

The central question throughout his 'Critique of Pure Reason,' revolves around the quest for knowledge or rather, 'Can there be certain knowledge?' **Kant** insisted that 'although our knowledge emanates from sense experience, it is not to be presumed that it emerges from experience.' **Kant** desired to discover 'the *a priori* conditions of all scientific knowledge' more eagerly than the knowledge gained from sense experience.

There are two distinct types of *a priori* knowledge, one type consisting of *analytic* propositions and the other type *synthetic* propositions. This distinction had been recognised by **Leibniz** who separated 'truths of fact' from 'truths of reason,' and by **Hume** who separated 'matters of fact' from 'relations between ideas.'

Kant affirmed that an *analytic* proposition is one in which the predicate is covertly present in the subject. For example, MPs are politicians. A *synthetic*proposition is different in this manner, the predicate is not present in the subject but connected to it. For example, MPs are inconsistent. All the propositions derived from our experience are 'synthetic.' Sense experience is the precondition for the birth and development of an empirical proposition. However, although sense experience may also give birth to an *a priori* proposition, its development is related to a factor independent of sense experience. The proposition 'one divided by one equals one' has no requirement for verification, so via analogy, we can accept that all the propositions of mathematics are of the *apriori* type.

The past perennial problem of discovering certain knowledge prompted **Kant** to focus the problem in this light, 'How are synthetic *a priori* judgements possible?' **Kant** claimed that the external world is the cause of human sensations, but the human internal world arranges these sensations in space and time.

Kant listed four transcendent ideas that cause perplexity.

1

Thesis

The world has, as to space and time, a beginning (limit)

Antithesis

The world is, as to space and time, infinite

2

Thesis

Everything in the world is constituted out of the simple

Antithesis

In the world, nothing is simple, but everything is composite

3
Thesis
In the world, there are causes through freedom

Antithesis
There is no freedom, for all is nature

4
Thesis
In the series of world-causes, there is some necessary being

Antithesis
In this series, all is contingent, there is nothing necessary

'The antimony, not arbitrarily invented but is found in the nature of human reason, and hence unavoidable.' Now, the 'Law of Contradiction' states that a proposition and its negation cannot both be true. In these four cosmological ideas, how is it possible to prove which proposition is true? Hence, antimony involves contradiction.

Georg Hegel insisted that knowledge has a journey of three stages. The first stage is where there is consciousness of the object by sense experience. The second stage is where there is a critical analysis of the senses reflecting on their deceptive nature, so here, knowledge is solely subjective. The third stage is where the subject and the object are conjoined, thereby assuming self-knowledge as the trunk of the tree of knowledge. For **Hegel**, all knowledge is that possessed by the Absolute, as the Absolute is the whole and contains all the parts. **Hegel** maintained that it is only via an objective mind which enables things in the universe to be comprehended.

It is significant to mention **Hegel's** 'Philosophy of History' due to its influence upon another philosopher. He declared that world history is connected with the application of the *dialectic,* demonstrating that from the thesis, the Oriental World, and the antithesis, the Classical World, emerged the Germanic World. He wrote: 'The only thought which philosophy brings with it to the contemplation of history is the simple conception of reason; that the history of the world, therefore, presents us with a rational process.' He believed that the development of the human spirit is influenced by the philosophy of history, where introspective behaviour identifies the soul as containing three indispensable ideals—the ideal of the beautiful, the ideal of God, and the ideal of truth, consecutively related to art, religion and philosophy.

Karl Marx developed his philosophy of history from the process conceived by **Hegel**, although originating from **Plato**, namely, the *dialectic.* However, whereas **Hegel** conceived the dialectical process as a spiritual process, **Marx** dogmatised that it was a materialistic process; matter is the ultimate reality and physical forces in the universe bring about change tempered by the dialectical process. Also, societies tend to conform to a sort of materialistic determinism, where the production of goods is controlled by powerful forces.

In the 'Communist Manifesto,' it is proclaimed, 'All history is the history of the class struggle.' **Marx** believed that a synthesis would emerge from the owners of the means of production and the employees producing the goods. **Marx** claimed that the doctrine of dialectical materialism is related to a process which will ultimately force a system to emerge that will govern human affairs. It requires a broad stretch of imagination to believe that inanimate matter can influence the stuff of history. Whereas **Hegel** was concerned with man's relation to spirit, **Marx** was obsessed by man's relation to matter.

Auguste Comte, a Frenchman, was not interested in the course of history; he was interested in expounding and applying scientific method. He was concerned with six concepts of things—being real, useful, certain, precise, organic and relative. In association with these concepts, he introduced the term *positive,* and he insisted that the method could be used in human affairs.

Comte was mainly concerned with knowledge that could be used to fertilise the growth of materialism which implies that scientific knowledge is the superior knowledge. He claimed that the scientific spirit emerged from three stages;

(i)   the mythical or theological stage;
(ii)   the abstract or metaphysical stage; and
(iii)   the concrete or positive stage.

He wanted precise answers and he contended that 'scientific method' provided the means to acquire the answers. Scientific method employs the 'triad' of observation, hypothesis (if this, then what?), and experiment; sometimes the results are accepted as *laws,* but more probably *rules.*

Comte's philosophy was extended by the 'Vienna circle,' or 'logical positivists' as they were known. Without doubt, this group of philosophers contrived a paradoxical predicament. The human intellect having struggled for centuries to establish and transmit the ideas of the good, the true and the beautiful, and having pressed for an education system to encourage a high regard for these values, then subscribed to a philosophy which proclaimed that such values are the result of mere speculation.

William James advised that the best procedure is to ignore the elusiveness of 'abstract truth' and consider the effects of action. **James** maintained that thinking is solely confined to solving our problems, so that our theories become *instruments* instead of answers to our problems. Now, prior to accepting or rejecting any philosophical doctrine, **James** wanted to know the 'cash-value' of the doctrine. In other words, what use had the doctrine and what is the benefit if it is true. In his book called *Pragmatism,* he wrote this controversial sentence, 'An idea is true so long as to believe it is profitable to our lives.'

In calling the sentence controversial, many problems have no cash-value, therefore according to **James**, the problems are not worth considering. Of course, this eliminates theological as well as metaphysical problems; this is consistent with his doctrine as he considered mind as another form of the material world. The judgement that the employment of any theory is to react from experience forms the essence of *Pragmatism,* 'what works is true.' The word *Pragmatism* was introduced by an American philosopher, **CS Peirce** who appreciated the difference between a scientific concept like force and an emotional concept like fear. **Peirce** was a disciple of 'Positivism' and his belief was the reverse of **James**, namely, 'what is true works.' In his conviction, if anything is true, then it cannot fail to work. The communist system has failed to work; therefore, the theory is not true. The question arises, 'Does the capitalist system work?' Before too quick a judgement is made, it must be decided if such a question is considered in the short term or the long term.

Charles Darwin was the author of the illustrious or maybe notorious work called 'The Origin of Species.' The adjectives are used because his theory has had a devastating impact upon society. **Darwin's** theory was divided into two significant parts:

(i)   the theory of evolution and
(ii)   the theory of natural selection.

The first theory is based upon the idea that different forms of life have evolved, by modification of structure from cruder forms, related to changes in the environment. Natural selection is the process by which plants and animals reproduce. Chance plays an important part in determining that those most suited to contend with their environment survive, whilst those which are least adaptive to their environment have the least chance to survive. **Darwin** provided the information for many impressionable men to become atheists. At that time, the doctrines of science had a far greater influence than the doctrines of theology. It certainly had a great influence on **Karl Marx** who proclaimed, '**Darwin's** book is important, and it serves me as a natural scientific basis for the class struggle in history.' Unfortunately, the doctrine of the 'survival of the fittest' was not just related to biology; it also included nations. Of course, **Darwin** never asked the question, 'What makes a being human so distinct from an animal?'

The last sixty years have seen the worst period of violence in the whole history of human affairs; spiritual values have been mocked, so demoralisation and dehumanisation was inevitable. The technological advances have led to a retreat to barbarism. In rejecting God in his unverifiable theory, **Darwin** near his death, confessed, "The consequences for the future of mankind were incalculable." This statement contradicted his prediction in the 'Origin of Species,' which claimed that man's 'mental endowment will tend to progress to perfection.'

Existing society appears to adhere to a firm belief in the material world, therefore society values scientific knowledge more than metaphysics. This is the intellectual tragedy of at least the last half century. Many believe that science establishes 'truth.' It is a false belief; science establishes part truth; it cannot establish full truth. Mathematics and physics cannot deal with the problem of good and evil or other similar problems.

'Meta' is the Greek word meaning 'after,' so metaphysics simply means 'after physics.' Hence, metaphysics is concerned with problems beyond the physical world. The central topic of metaphysics is *ontology,* which involves the study of BEING or all that exists; material objects, minds, concepts, facts, values, numbers, time, space, God etc. Metaphysics is the indispensable source of knowledge to the understanding of the meaning and purpose of all life.

Any history of knowledge ought to include the traditional conception of nature as a **great chain of being,** which is an ascent from the lowest to the highest level of being. Sir **Richard Blackmore** and **John Hughes** declared in their *Lay Monastery:*

44

Nothing is more surprising and delightful than to observe the Scale or the gradual Ascent from Minerals to Plants, from Plants to Animals, and from Animals to Human Beings. It is easy to perceive these Kinds until you come to the highest of one, and the lowest of that next above it; and then the difference tends to perplex the curious and to humble the proud philosopher.

In the hierarchic structure of BEING, there are factors which grade one type of being higher than another. The lowest level of being is mineral, or a chemical element or a compound. What is the chief characteristic of all minerals? All are inanimate, that is, destitute of life or spirit. The ascent to the next level of being involves the change from the inorganic to the organic. Soil contains a host of living organisms and the knowledge of its entire nature is elusive. In plants, we notice a significant change in level of being; plants have a life force and the property to grow. These powers also exist in animals, hut an additional power is evident, consciousness. Knock an animal unconscious, then it is in a similar state to a plant but devoid of movement. The ascent to a higher level of being normally reveals a state of consciousness and intelligence upon maturity. At this level, a mysterious power is available, namely, the power of being conscious of its own consciousness. When this power is neglected, there is a tendency to exist at a lower level of being. Finally, the highest level of being is Divine Being as shown on the chart of the **Chain of Being.**

----

sovereign good
Divine Being
Wisdom

Values
Human Being
self-knowledge
self-interest

Animal
Consciousness
survival

Plant
Life-force
living organisms

Soil
Organic
chemical elements

Mineral
Inorganic

Levels of being reveal the meaning and purpose of human existence and to exclude contemplation of levels of being can be deduced as sheer bigotry. Things that are true in the world of animals and human beings are non-existent in the world of minerals, like the emotion of fear. At each level of being, the environment becomes more complex. Can we believe that a socio-cultural environment exists in a lower level of being?

The notion of Being is also associated with the movement of **existentialism.** This group of contemporary philosophers have varied ideas on religion, politics and philosophy. Existentialists are fervently interested in the programme of human existence and they have followed the lead set by **Martin Heidegger,** who contrasted the kind of being that men experience with the kind of being that applies to things.

Soren Kierkegaard raised the question, 'What is the point of man's life?' He believed that there must be some form of communication between man and God, yet it is impossible to prove the existence of God. The meaning of human existence is not discovered by knowledge but by *enlightenment.* Man has no other option than to have 'faith.'

Jean-Paul Sartre accepted **Kierkegaard's** portrayal of the human predicament but rejected his claim that there was no other option than to have faith. According to **Sartre**, human beings live in a meaningless world and when they do not escape from things, they live in 'bad faith.'

Existentialists emphasise that human beings are active and creative whereas things are not. Things remain as they are but men do not have to remain the same. Human beings have a free choice, although some assert, before they choose, they must choose the principles on which they choose. Human beings must accept the reality of their 'dreadful freedom,' they are free to choose their destiny and change their way of life, but they are responsible for their choice.

Some existentialists have disparaged past philosophers and accused them of wasting their time in ignoring the real problems of human existence. Language and logic cannot solve certain human problems. Such problems cannot be solved, they can only be transcended by the intervention of a concept of a higher level of being, like wisdom or love. If valid reason can supply no solution to the problems implicated in human existence, then the only alternative is faith. The question cannot be evaded, 'Faith in what?'

Chapter 3
Logic and Language

A dictionary may possibly give the meaning of *logic* as the 'science of reasoning,' but there is valid and invalid reasoning. Therefore, logic relates to a special type of thinking. Ever since **Aristotle** projected the image of a human being as a 'rational animal,' many have asserted that the distinctive nature of human beings is their ability to think, but according to **Gilbert Ryle,** 'thinking' is a 'polymorphous' concept. What is this type of concept? Building is a perfect example of a polymorphous concept, which may admit only one or all the diverse activities of builders; trenching prior to the laying of foundations and drains mortar mixing and brick laying, joinery, roofing, glazing, plastering, tiling, plumbing, as well as electrical and gas installations. The activities with the concept of building are so varied compared with the concept of 'sleeping.'

The inevitable conclusion is that 'thinking' is a polymorphous concept which includes different types of activity. In autistic thinking, there is no commanding interest and an absence of goal-directed behaviour. Fantasy thinking, idle thinking or day-dreaming is an activity which psychologists maintain is an expression of imagination related to unfulfilled wishes, needs and desires. The statement, 'I cannot think' is sometimes uttered instead of the statement, 'I cannot remember.' 'Thinking' and 'believing' sometimes present confusion about their meaning. 'Thinking' normally involves the construction of an argument, whereas 'believing' normally expresses a subjective opinion, attitude or moral judgement.

There is a significant type of thinking that bypasses the free emissions from autistic thinking and the efficient control of memory; the type is known as imaginative thinking. Reflective thinking is the antithesis of autistic thinking, as each association disclosed is commanded by an intensity of interest as well as by goal-directed behaviour, which tends to dominate during the whole activity.

Therefore, 'thinking' may be defined as a type of dispositional behaviour, and as **Gilbert Ryle** indicated, it responds to the prescription of 'drills and skills.' So, by the application of 'drills and skills,' analogical thinking together with analytical thinking pave the way for the emergence of the *model*.

In a real sense, two types of thinking exist, infirm thinking and intense thinking. Autistic thinking is a definite case of infirm thinking, but generally, when a person roves from one topic to another, rambles hither and thither, and refuses to dwell upon a certain question, preferring the licence of 'mind-wandering;' this is a common case of infirm thinking. The intense thinking process is a sort of vacillation between two points of contact, the realistic and the imaginative.

If we start a critical examination of our own beliefs, then we are sure to discover that some of them are devoid of a concrete basis. Many of our beliefs have originated from another person claiming that a certain proposition is true. In other words, we have merely assumed a proposition is true without any reason for supposing it is true. Many of our beliefs exist through self-interest which is related to our means of earning a living or the way of acquiring wealth. We accept and adhere to some beliefs because it pays us to behave in this way; we benefit by such action conforming to our belief.

Self-interest is also identified with status or popularity with one's neighbours, friends, church, political organisation or social club; the relationship is dependent upon maintaining certain beliefs. A personal career is another significant factor where self-interest dominates; the world of politics is the classic example. Political careers and business enterprise pursued by persons may unconsciously force them to become a slave to a false belief. A person may truly say that he or she enjoys the activities of the rat-race, so is he or she free from bondage?

It becomes manifest that the existing situation is far from ideal with respect to logic, therefore **Gilbert Ryle'ue** s advice on 'drills and skills' must be accepted. The habit ought to be developed where every proposition may be challenged by subjecting it to three questions:

(i)   How do we know about this proposition?

(ii)   What reasons or reason have we for accepting this proposition?

(iii)   What is the evidence and where was it obtained to support this proposition?

Propositions and beliefs may be accepted to be true from the conclusion of:

(i)   the judgement of the first person or

(ii)   the judgement of a third person. With respect to (ii) the judgement of a third person, the first person must have reasoned confidence in the third person, so, it is necessary to examine the ability of the judge as well as the judgement. If the judge fails the examination, then there can be no reasoned confidence.

Without introducing metaphysics in which the major topic is 'being,' the definition of fact reduces to a tautology. In answer to **Pontius Pilate's** question, 'What is truth?' the truth about any belief is that it corresponds to fact. What is fact? Fact is that which is without dependence on sense-perception or belief. There are three methods by which facts may be discovered:

(i)   by perception (sense-data)

(ii)   by inference (reasoning) or

(iii)   by intuition (direct relation).

We know by direct perception that the sun is a source of light and heat. However, it is only by inference that we know why the sun rises and sets. Inference or reasoning is a technique of thinking which enables us to ascertain if the conclusion of an argument is true or false. The conclusion is derived from the truth of other propositions which provide the proof. *Deductive Logic* has been defined as 'valid reasoning,' yet really, it is the process to infer a valid conclusion from a posed proposition or a set of propositions.

Stranger than fiction is the repetitive case of a remarkable statement that has not been restricted to any social class. Few cannot have encountered the statement, 'That may be alright in theory, but it doesn't work out in practice.' So, the immediate conclusion to be drawn is that failure to work out in practice means the theory is false. Hence, theory has been viewed with scepticism. No theory is true unless it is in accord with all the relevant facts. Such a common case denotes a misconception about the meaning of the word 'theory.'

All valid reasoning or intensive thinking mainly consists of the formulation and verification of a theory or hypothesis. It is beyond the scope of this book to continue towards the complex nature of *probability theory* or the *calculus of chances,* but the induction method cannot be excluded. There is a subtle relation between a law, a hypothesis and a theory. A law is established if it is accepted, independent of whether it is true. However, a hypothesis is the result of observations but it is not accepted, even though it may be true. A theory consists of one or more hypotheses which are either true or false. Sometimes, confusion arises about the distinction between *laws of nature* and *natural law.* The laws of nature are synonymous with the laws of science. Natural law is synonymous with the moral law or laws derived from the general nature of the universe, acquired solely by reason devoid of any appeal to revelation.

A proposition is really a statement wherein the subject affirms or denies the predicate. Questions (Interrogative), wishes or desires (Optative), or commands (Imperative) that form a sentence do not count as propositions. To form a proposition means reducing the principal verb in the sentence to the present tense of the verb 'to be,' namely, 'is' or 'are,' which is called the *copula.*

A proposition may be 'affirmative,' that is, declares to be true, or 'negative,' denies to be true. When the word 'all' or 'no' and equivalent words are used, then it is a universal proposition. When the word 'some' or 'few' or an equivalent word is used, then it is a particular proposition. A universal proposition or a particular proposition may be either affirmative or negative. 'All men are fools' is an illustration of a universal affirmative proposition. 'Some men are not fools' is an illustration of a particular negative preposition.

Loosely, logic may be described as deep thinking about ideas that can be justified by valid reasoning. All departments of philosophy involve the intensive thinking process, but the flower of any system of philosophy must be pollinated by the laws of logic. Continuing the metaphor, the tree of knowledge has two deep roots, one called *formal logic* and the other, *logical theory.* The two main rational processes are *deduction* and *induction.* The difference between the two processes is clear in the examples; deduction—all x's are y's; induction—all observed x's are y's, so all x's are y's, and all=100%.

Deductive logic contains an argument whereby a conclusion is drawn from certain premises, obeying the principle that not to accept the conclusion predetermines a false premise. On the other hand, inductive logic is confined to an argument whereby from certain premises, a conclusion is drawn directly from the evidence. The traditional form of inductive logic is as follows: 'All observed crows are black; therefore, all crows are black.' Of course, if a white crow is ever observed, then the conclusion is false.

The *syllogism* constructed by Aristotle is the starting point to understand deductive logic. Loosely, it may be defined as an argument which consists of a conclusion deduced from two premises, therefore, only three propositions are required in any syllogism. The first and second propositions must be reasonable assertions or denials to provide the third proposition with the proof that the argument is valid.

Every proposition must commence with a 'quantifier' word followed by the 'subject expression' connected to or related to the 'predicate expression' by the 'cupola,' that is, 'is' or 'are.'

(i) All cats are animals.

(ii) All tigers are cats.

(iii) All tigers are animals.

Expressing the above example in symbolic form:

(i) All x are y

(ii) All z are x

(iii) All z are y

All the above propositions are universal-affirmative. If we made the first proposition, 'No fish are animals,' then the proposition is universal-negative. If we made the first proposition, 'Some cats are black animals,' therefore the proposition is particular-affirmative. If we made the first proposition, 'Some cats are not black animals,' the proposition is particular-negative.

To ensure that a syllogism has a valid form, there are three terms which must be appropriately placed, and each term is used only twice. The terms are known as the 'middle term,' 'major term,' and 'minor term.' In the latter example, x is the 'middle term,' y is the 'major term' and z is the 'minor term.' It can be seen that the first proposition contains y, the 'major term,' so it is called the 'major premise.' The second proposition contains z, the 'minor term,' so it is called the 'minor premise.' Also, both premises contain the 'middle term.' Obviously, the conclusion must contain the 'major term' and the 'minor term.' It is essential for any valid syllogism to comply with this form.

Let us consider why the following syllogism is false:

All sparrows are birds;
All robins are birds;
therefore, all robins are sparrows.

Both propositions are true, but the conclusion is false. The error in the syllogism is that the premises are not connected by the 'middle term.' This error in the structure of the syllogism is known as the 'fallacy of the undistributed middle.'

Let us consider why the following syllogism is false:

All Alsatians are animals;
All dogs are animals;
therefore, all Alsatians are dogs.

Both premises are true and the conclusion is true. However, the syllogism is false. By observing the major and minor terms in the conclusion, the middle term should be 'animals.' Really, there exist three separate propositions with no connecting 'middle term.' The error is synonymous with the previous error, the argument does not distribute its 'middle term.'

Let us consider why the following syllogism is false:

No politicians are liars;
No liars are saints:
therefore, no politicians are saints.

When the premises are two negative propositions, there is no connection between the major and minor terms. To prove that 'No politicians are liars,' we must prove that 'politicians are liars,' which is an affirmative proposition contradicting the 'major premise.' Hence, in any syllogism, no conclusion can be drawn from two negative premises. Why is this syllogism false?

All genocide is wrong;
Some surgery is not wrong;
therefore, some surgery is genocide.

The major premise is affirmative and the minor premise is negative, so the middle term is distributed correctly. However, although the premises are true, the conclusion is false, since it is presumed that if 'some surgery is not wrong,' therefore, 'some surgery is wrong.' The rule affirms that the conclusion must be negative whenever either premise is negative.

The previous syllogism would be true if it conformed to the schemata of *Camestres*.

All y is x.
No z is x.
No z is y.

There are five important rules for defining the validity or invalidity of a syllogistic argument. They relate to whether a proposition is affirmative or negative, and to the distribution of expressions.

(i)   The distribution of the middle term is required at least once or twice.
(ii) If the distribution of a term is absent in the premises, then its distribution must be absent in the conclusion.
(iii) Two negative premises do not permit a conclusion to be drawn.
(iv) One negative premise demands the conclusion to be negative.
(v)   Two affirmative premises do not permit the conclusion to be negative.

Irrespective of the schemata and rules, the premises must be tested for validity or invalidity, for only if the premises are true can the conclusion be verified as true.

Invalid arguments may occur for three reasons.

(i)   The argument may be formally fallacious, in other words, inconsistent with the syllogistic criteria.
(ii) The argument may contain a false premise.
(iii) The argument may be irrelevant or circular, whereby the invalid reasoning is directly linked to content rather than attached to syllogistic criteria. Such arguments are known as informal fallacies; some of the most common are listed on the next page.

Whenever the conclusion is adopted or presupposed by a premise, there emerges the fallacy of 'circular reasoning.'

> If politics is corrupt, citizens should not vote;
> But citizens should vote,
> So, politics is not corrupt.

Whenever an attack is mounted against a person instead of the person's belief or opinion, so as to reveal falsehood, then the fallacy of *argumentum ad homminem* is committed. Lawyers and politicians frequently employ this fallacy in attempting to discredit a witness or opponent rather than producing facts to support their argument. Sometimes, this argument is referred to as 'abusing the man.'

When it is argued that the lack of evidence approving or disapproving a claim must be accepted as evidence, then the fallacy of *argumentum ignoraratium* is committed. This vulgar argument is better known as the fallacy of 'appealing to ignorance.'

An argument which attempts to prove something but instead proves something else so that the exponent appears to be ignorant of the question; this fallacy was exposed by **Aristotle** and every case of *ignoratio elenchi* is an irrelevant appeal.

When an irrelevant appeal to pity is used to influence a person to accept or to act upon a particular principle by arousing that person's sympathy or compassion, then the fallacy of *argumentum admisericordiam* is committed.

When pride is used to influence a person to accept an opinion, it is yet another irrelevant appeal. Typical examples are: 'You should be proud of your country.' 'You should be proud of your government's achievements.'

When humour is introduced to divert attention from the question, the fallacy of 'humorous confusion' is committed. Especially in politics, too frequently humorous references are substituted for valid criticism. In the House of Commons, an opposition spokesman is more inclined to say, 'This is more hysterical than hypothetical.'

When anger is employed to upset an opponent's self-composure, then the common fallacy of 'confusion by anger' is committed. Insults and innuendo when employed usually result in the confusion of the argument by inciting anger.

Accepting the Machiavellian Principle, that is, every means may be employed to attain a desired end; this is known as the fallacy of the 'end justifies the means.' The aim to eradicate the AIDS disease is important, but it would be an act of barbarism to eliminate all carriers. As a general statement, the 'end justifies the means' is unacceptable, and in rational politics, the end is associated with social well-being.

History records that the stagnant state of 'logic' was finally recognised, and it was the destiny of **Sir William Hamilton** to highlight the obstinacy of philosophers who accepted the logic of **Aristotle** as the alpha and omega of the theory. Without a shadow of doubt, the critical spotlight hovered over the false assumption of **Immanuel Kant** who proclaimed that logic 'to all appearances has reached its conclusion.' This closed and locked attitude was forced open by **Hamilton's** insistence that 'many valid forms of judgement and reasoning in ordinary use, but which the ancient logic continued to ignore, are now openly recognised as legitimate; and many *relations* which hitherto lay hid, now come forward into the light.'

Hamilton's main contribution to the development of logic, although not spectacular, generated the chink of light enabling progress in logic to reach beyond **Aristotle's** dreams. **Hamilton** changed the four forms of the syllogistic schemata; he achieved this by the 'quantification of the predicate.'

Thus, the form of Barbara, 'all x are y' is changed to 'all x are all y;' the form of *Celarent*, 'no x are y' is changed to 'no x are no y;' the form of *Disamis*, 'some x are y' is changed to 'some x are some y;' the form of *Bocardo*, 'some x are not y' is changed to 'some x are not some y.' Previously, the predicate had no 'sign of quantity' connected to it, whereas in **Hamilton's** logic, a 'sign of quantity' is connected.

It is easy to perceive that a proposition becomes an equation of its subject and predicate. By reducing propositions to equations, it gives the impression that the system of logic is merely the formation of equations. **Hamilton's** action amounted to getting rid of the verb 'to be' and replacing it with the 'sign of equality.' However, all the time algebraic symbols were treated as signs of quantities, progress was restricted. Logic and algebra are not analogical as algebraic symbols are always associated with quantities or operations involving addition or subtraction. The obsession with quantities was a condition that demanded treatment to maintain progress in logic.

Augustus de Morgan made the copula (is or are) and the sign of addition subject to a more flexible arrangement. In the algebraic equation x+y=y+x, it became recognised that it is not necessary for x and y to remain as quantities, which meant that x and y could be replaced by something else on the condition that it obeyed the law. **De Morgan** suggested the plus sign could signify 'tied to,' so if x is tied to y, then y is tied to x, but the equation is still valid.

Consider the rule: x is y and y is z, then x is z; only one proposition can be accepted as true. However, if we change the copula from 'is affirmable of,' or 'is identical to,' or 'is in agreement with' to a transitive relation such as *believing,* then by substitution we obtain, x believes y and y believes z, then x believes z. Can any of the transitive relations be accepted as true? **De Morgan** argued that we can substitute the copula by any symbol showing the kind of relation existing between the subject and predicate.

The significant progress made in contemporary logic was due to the *logic of relations,* so **De Morgan** was justified in claiming that 'here the general notion of relations emerges, and for the first time in the history of knowledge, the notion of relation and *relation of relations* are symbolised.' Traditional logic clinging to the function of the copula could not account for the following elementary reasoning process: 'Three exceeds two and two exceeds one, thus, three exceeds one.' Obviously, the main verb indicates a relation between the subject and predicate. This advance in logical theory led to the decline of classical logic with its attachment to the syllogism, which is now considered to be included in the *predicate calculus.*

George Boole was a mathematician who devised a logic of algebra which defied ordinary algebraic laws. In his algebra of 'classes,' he argued that if we pick out objects from a certain class, and then pick out objects from our selected objects forming a private class, all the objects stay in a certain class with no change in quantity. The mathematician explained by symbolic interpretation as shown:

$$X \times X = X$$
$$\text{Or } x^2 = x$$

The equation is unbalanced and therefore patently wrong. This false equation was no handicap to **George Boole** who quite literally pursued a method to make a false equation into a true equation. His method compelled him to introduce a quantities interpretation. If the law is made whereby x can only equal either 0 or 1, then it can be seen that **George Boole** worked the oracle.

This fundamental equation became the springboard for the analogical development of the 'laws of thought' with the laws of a 'dual algebra.' It enabled **Boole** to delve into the method of constructing and analysing general statements by converting them into equations.

Besides this indispensable contribution to the development of mathematical logic, **Boole** attempted to employ symbolic logic in the calculation of probabilities which is our red light. Before stopping entirely, it is important to mention that in digital techniques, we make use of a sequential logic circuit which possesses the property of memory.

Consider a switch which can make or break an electrical circuit; it can be ON or NOT ON. Now, the Boolean variables 1 and 0 represent ON or NOT ON, and are used in conjunction with the functions of AND and OR as well as NAND and NOR. The last two words meaning NOT AND and NOT OR. Circuits which involve combinational logic are known as gates which include AND, OR, NAND, NOR and one other gate, all of which have circuit properties that are shown via the Boolean symbol in their truth-table. Cause and effect prompted the extension of the discussion to reveal a major development since **Boole**, but we are swimming into deep water when discussing the application of digital techniques underlying the digital computer.

It is valid to raise the question at this point—can logic help in solving problems? Logic provides us with a method whereby the validity or invalidity of a conclusion may be drawn from its premises. However, logic provides no means to verify any of our ultimate premises, or to demonstrate that the premises are meaningful. Formal logic merely lays down the ground rules and the appropriate form for assertions to be tested.

On many occasions, an argument centres on two-valued logic in which true and false are recognised as the two acceptable truth values. A red rose is either red or not red. A human being is either rational or irrational on occasions. The universe was either created or not created. A government is either just or unjust. In all the previous examples, a definite distinction is sought so that a 'degree of truth' is inconsistent with the two truth-values.

There are certainly cases where a two-valued logic is justified, like when affirming that the following statement is false, 'Roses are vegetables.' On the other hand, there are many cases where we infer that a 'degree of truth' prevails and this inference is expressed in appropriate language. In a set of circumstances, which factor should dominate and to what extent, justice or mercy? Too much justice becomes tyranny, and too much mercy beckons anarchy. Of course, the concepts of justice and mercy must be subject to a common understanding, but unfortunately, two-valued logic cannot help.

Aristotle was prompted to undertake an extensive enquiry into the processes of reasoning which may have been influenced by the proposition of **Socrates**, 'All men are mortal.' The proposition results from the method of induction by observing that all men of previous generations have died, so it is induced that all men encounter death. Whereas his tutor **Plato**, used the dialectic method or the art of reason, **Aristotle** formulated the deductive method. His science of reason contains the logical laws of 'identity,' 'contradiction' and 'excluded middle,' which were instinctively called the 'Laws of Thought.'

The 'Law of Identity' states, *whatever is, is.*
The 'Law of Contradiction' states, Nothing can both be and not be.
The 'Law of Excluded Middle' states, All things must either be or not be.

The 'Law of Identity' in symbolised form is self-evident; all x is x. However, **John Hospers** recognised the difficulty, 'What are you saying about a statement when you declare that its truth is self-evident?' The 'Law of Contradiction' states that a proposition and its denial cannot both be true; in symbolised form; not both x or not x. The 'Law of Excluded Middle' states that every proposition is either true or false because each thing either holds or lacks any particular property, or in symbolised form, either x or not x. As the statements of logic go far beyond the statements about numbers or symbols, we must be certain that a logical law is incontestable.

Unfortunately, the 'Law of Excluded Middle' has been found to be fallacious. The law states, 'Either x or not x.' Are we correct in assuming the speed of a motor vehicle is either fast or slow; then what is average speed? A problem is highlighted, 'Can the laws of logic be used to establish the laws of logic?' This is the logical predicament; the ultimate laws of logic cannot be proved to be true, since to attempt such an exercise is to beg the question, for the proof established by the conclusion has already been established in the original proposition.

Aristotle's insistence that any proposition must contain a subject-copula-predicate, however, the syllogism introduced a problem about two types of propositions. If it is said, 'Politics is the art of government,' there can be no doubt that this is an objective statement. However, suppose it is said, 'Politics is a dirty business, it can be construed as a subjective opinion which may be either false or true.'

Logic helps us to study the results of thought; it cannot help us to study the processes of thought in struggling with problems.

HE Durkin suggested that there are 3 stages in problem-solving behaviour.

(i)   The nature of the problem must be recognised, then the activity of the mind is introduced.

(ii) Investigation of the cause of the problem exists is the next stage after recognition.

(iii) Analysis of the problem using the information obtained from recognition and investigation.

(iv) Struggling with the problem; first by solving parts of the problem before the solution of the whole problem is obtained. Emotional reaction via frustration, anxiety, anger or disappointment can have a direct effect on the problem-solving efficiency.

Durkin pointed out that these four phases are flexible as the fourth phase struggling with the problem may involve different patterns of behaviour. One pattern is 'insighted behaviour,' a person who has insight to a problem knows the nature of the problem; what is required and has an idea that will solve the problem. Another pattern relates to 'trial and error' in order to discover a clue leading to the solution of the problem. Finally, the typical philosopher's pattern of behaviour is inextricably linked to the 'analytical approach;' it is an approach that includes insight, trial and error and valid reasoning.

Language or the expression of ideas by words has been one of the most important steps in the journey from barbarism to civilisation. Language is a means for reflective thinking and communication. When in the reflective mode, a person may use words in any manner for convenience, but as soon as a person has a relationship or becomes engaged in communication, then another person arrives on the scene. When the first person contacts the second person, it involves using words or sentences to convey meaning. Words are either uttered or written by the first person hoping the second person understands them. Efficient communication is achieved only if the second person's understanding is synonymous with the first person's meaning. The essential thing is that persons use the same words for the same things and meaning.

Ludwig Wittgenstein was the founder of a sort of method showing philosophical perplexity is the result of confusion about how language operates. When a child learns a language, there is a slow development to think within its system. The child had no pre-knowledge of the language with which to converse and understand. In the simple multiplication of numbers, does the child become aware of the process before or after the act of multiplying. The comparison of thinking with experience points to the fact that an experience we pass has a passive nature whereas real thinking has an active nature. Therefore, the comparison of thoughts is unlike the comparison of experiences. If language and thought are combined, then language is not absorbed in thought since it cannot be discovered beforehand in the mind. It has been argued that thought is a form of symbol manipulation, however, meaning requires explanation.

Objects that are around us in our sensible world are all identified by words. When a builder is teaching an apprentice his trade, he must explain the meaning and difference between a brick, a block, a lintel, a strut, a tie and a beam. Obviously, the apprentice is compelled to 'learn the names of the objects' which are the basics in the construction of language. However, the meaning of a word is related to its use in the language rather than the object that it names. The meaning of a word is understood when anyone knows how to use it. The description of the use of words is more important than interpreting the words as names. A child learns to read books and ride a bicycle rather than just to learn that there exist books and bicycles.

Wittgenstein observed that just as the grammar of language emerged long after the language had been used for the purpose of communication, primitive games were also played without a single rule having been formulated for the purpose of fairness. For **Wittgenstein**, 'Systems of communication' are nothing more than 'language games,' and a simple, primitive language can be referred to as a language game. If a student studies technical subjects which include a special vocabulary, and involves the use of diagrams, graphical representation with symbols, then more language games are learned.

Wittgenstein emphasised that the activity of reflection takes place in the compass of a language game and such a game is not devised from the activity of reflection. Therefore, all modes of reasoning can only take place in the compass of a language game; 'The chains of reason come to an end, to wit, on the boundary of the game.' The language game must be considered as something unperceived, devoid of any foundation, neither reasonable nor unreasonable.

In his *Philosophical investigations* this statement was made by **Wittgenstein**, 'If the language games are changed, the concepts are changed, and with the concept the meaning of words.' He maintained that in seeking to explore outside of language man seeks to express what cannot be expressed. What he really meant is that man refuses to recognise the limitation of language.

It has been pointed out that **Wittgenstein** was more concerned about 'How human beings express,' rather than 'what human beings express.' **Wittgenstein** was an associate member of the Vienna School which pursued a closed-shop philosophy adhering to the belief that no statement of a metaphysical kind can be true or false; they are nonsensical or strictly meaningless. From this conviction, the famous 'verification principle' of the 'logical positivists' emerged. How any intelligent person can ignore the 'nature of being' and 'scale of being' is also nonsensical.

The philosophy of logical positivism was expressed most clearly by **Wittgenstein**.

Most propositions and questions that have been written about philosophical matters are not false but nonsensical. We cannot therefore answer questions of this kind at all, but only state their senselessness. A work of philosophy consists of entirely elucidation. The result of philosophy is not a number of philosophical propositions, but to make propositions clear. All propositions are of equal value, hence also there can be no ethical propositions.

It remains true, the motive to eliminate metaphysics was just nonsensical metaphysics; **Etienne Gilson** detected the error where metaphysics is excluded from the intellectual menu.

Before their unexpected success in finding conclusive explanations of the material world, men had begun to despise all disciplines in which such demonstrations could not be found, or to rebuild those disciplines after the pattern of the physical sciences. So, as a result metaphysics and ethics had to be ignored or, at least replaced by new positive sciences. A very dangerous move indeed, which accounts for the perilous position in which western culture has now found itself.

Chapter 4
God and Godlessness

Hamlet commenced his soliloquy on a future state with this question: 'To be or not to be? that is the question.' Accordingly, it is appropriate to commence this chapter in a similar manner: 'To believe or not to believe in the existence of God? that is the principal question.'

In the history of philosophy, there are various treatises to show that some philosophers believed that the existence of God can be verified by natural or rational evidence; others have argued that no such evidence can be found to justify belief in a divine being. Those who claimed that there is no valid proof for the existence of God fall into one of three categories:

(i)   *Atheism* involves a firm refusal to believe that a divine being exists; the existence of God is impossible to prove.

(ii)   *Agnosticism* involves the belief that nothing can be known about the existence of God. There is a lack of rational evidence to accept the existence or non-existence of a divine being.

(iii)   *Fideism* involves a firm refusal to believe that rational evidence can be obtained proving the existence of God. The rejection of any account of religious knowledge leads to the conclusion that *pure faith* is necessary to seek God.

Those who believe there is rational evidence proving the existence of God encounter the problem of the nature of God. The metaphysical question relating to Divine Will and Divine Intelligence has led to the development of three theories about the nature of God.

Pantheism is a theory which involves the belief that God is not a separate, independent being; all things in the universe relate either to God or Nature.

Deism is a theory contrary to most religious traditions. The existence of God is accepted, but God is devoid of any power to influence or control events which occur throughout the universe; prayer is pointless since no relationship is possible between any human being and a divine being. The classic example of *Deism* is the 19th Psalm, as paraphrased into verse by the essayist **Joseph Addison.**

The spacious firmament on high,
With all the blue ethereal sky,
And spangled heavens, a shining frame,
Their great original proclaim.
The unwearied sun, from day to day,
Does its Creator's power display;
And publishes to every land,
The work of a Divine hand.
Soon as the evening shades prevail
The moon takes up the wondrous tale,
And nightly to the listening earth,
Repeats the story of her birth;
Whilst all the stars around her burn,
And all the planets, in their turn,
Confirm the tidings as they roll,
And spread the truth from pole to pole.
What though in solemn silence all
Move round this dark terrestrial ball;
What though no real voice, nor sound,
Amidst their radiant orbs be found,
In reason's ear they all rejoice,
And utter forth a glorious voice,
For ever singing as they shine,
The HAND that made us is DIVINE.

Theism is a theory which involves a firm belief in the existence of God. Whether God has infinite power or knowledge is queried due to the evil events that occur on Earth. However, it is accepted that God has a positive or personal relationship with human beings and assists them in the struggle against evil. Without God's help, it is difficult to conquer evil.

In anthropology, we learn that man believed in many Gods rather than the belief in one God. Primitive man believed in Gods of the sky, the earth, the winds, the seas, fire, forests and scores of others. As time passed, man reduced the number of Gods to a few powerful deities. It was on top of Mount Sinai where God said to Moses: 'I am the Lord, thy God, which have brought thee out of the…house of bondage. Thou shalt have no other God before me.' Moses persuaded the Israelites not to fear this all-powerful God called Jehovah. Possibly, the reason they feared was related to Jehovah's warning, 'I am a jealous God.' This conversion to the belief in one God paved the way for universal acceptance.

Natural *Religion* contends that religious knowledge can be obtained without faith or revelation. It investigates the abilities and nature of God besides the possibility of an almighty deity. The orbit of religious experience revolves around faith and mysticism as there is a poverty of proof.

Natural *Theology* studies the existence and nature of God claiming that natural evidence is available to verify that God exists.

It is not clear whether **Plato** believed in one God or many Gods, for in the 'Timaeus,' he introduces a 'Demiurge' who supervised the construction of order out of the chaos in the universe from the ideas and material that pre-existed. From this viewpoint, no other conclusion can be drawn except that the universe was not created out of nothing by God. God installed divine reason in the soul which is contained in the human body, and it possesses the faculty of acquiring knowledge about the eternal things in the universe. **Plato** conceived God as a good God who created the universe from the design of the eternal; being without jealousy. A disagreement appears with the Hebrew God.

Aristotle's metaphysics reveals that the real principle of motion is always the end or the form; it posits the motion which the matter undergoes. Motion has always existed and always will exist. Now, time is related to motion, therefore time has always existed; therefore, there was no beginning. The end is above the principle; thus all reality intervenes between the first matter and the first Mover after whom everything strives. At the end of the striving is to realise a state of pure form, that is, form devoid of matter; there must be an ultimate cause of all motion yet remain motionless. The 'Unmoved Mover' is the Perfect Being and God's existence is the ultimate cause of man's striving.

The Stoics believed there is one God within the universe and insisted that there is one soul in the human body. Everything that happens in the universe is a part of God. The principle of Form which relates to soul, nature or Zeus was conceived as simulating fire. This fire which is the same as warmth was accepted as the true nature of the deity. It permits things to exit and return in alternating forms. The Stoic *pantheism* was accompanied by total fatalism, so that man is subject to an immutable fate.

In the first line of the gospel according to St John, we see the influence of Greek philosophy through the *logos* which is associated with **Plato's** belief that everything in the universe is a copy of an idea in the mind of God. **Philo,** who was a Jewish philosopher, attempted to reconcile Greek philosophy with Hebrew scriptures by re-affirming that God is the source of everything that exists in the universe. God is a stranger to matter, but inferring from the order in matter, in other words, a cause of that matter, then God is identified as the orderer of the universe. As there is a refusal by God to act directly upon matter, an intermediary is available like a spiritual instrument through which the order posited by God enters into matter. This spiritual instrument is the *logos* interpreted as either the Word or Wisdom of God.

Plotinus completes the series of philosophers of antiquity and he borrowed from **Plato** to construct his mystical doctrine. **Plotinus** conceived a Trinity different from the Christian Trinity; the One, both God and Good is 'infinite being;' next in the Trinity is *nous* meaning 'intellectual spirit' and it is the image of the One; finally, there is Soul which is a part of a universal Soul. Originally, the human soul belonged to the pure universal Soul, but it was attracted by matter, thus causing it to break away to fulfil its desire to have a relationship with matter. The Soul must divorce itself from matter, and when succeeding, it will return to God where it was first domiciled.

Apologists for Christianity opposed to Judaism and heathenism were the first to recognise that philosophy has merit and ceased to brand it as heresy. The most important of the *Apologists* was **Justin** who refuted the slanders against the doctrine of Christianity. He developed the doctrine of the *Divine logos* which works in every rational being and became flesh in Jesus Christ; it extended the doctrine of the Fall, which proceeded from the will; the doctrine of original sin resulting from the Fall, and finally, the doctrine of New Birth.

Origen said that there is nothing wholly incorporeal except God-Father, Son and Holy Ghost. The doctrine of the Trinity which claims the genesis of the Son is eternal was certainly influenced by the Trinity of **Plotinus. Origen** argued that anyone who transferred his attention from Greek philosophy to the Gospels would conclude that they are true; 'the Gospel has a demonstration of its own, more divine than any established by Grecian dialectics.'

Anyone who undertakes a study of the Christian creeds will be surprised by the number that were compiled. Such confessions of faith emerged in connection with the rite of baptism. The development of the Christian creeds relates to **Tertullian** who gave a citation of the rule of faith. This led to the set form of the creed. **Tertullian** was the originator of *trinitas,* 'three persons in one substance.'

The third and fourth centuries were critical periods in the history of the Catholic Church. After **Tertullian's** citation, declaratory creeds became a common practice and each local church formed its own creed. One of the local creeds which was to have a profound influence has been identified as the Old Roman baptismal creed, and can be traced to the end of the second century. The Old Roman creed is extremely significant as it embraces the creed of the Apostles and the following has been extracted from the manuscript, *Codex Antiquissimus:*

> *I believe in God the Father almighty; and in Christ Jesus His only Son, our Lord, Who was born from the Holy Spirit and the Virgin Mary, Who under Pontius Pilate was crucified and buried, on the third day rose again from the dead, ascended to heaven, sits on the right hand of the Father, whence he will come to judge the living and the dead; and in the Holy Spirit, the holy church, the remission of sins, the resurrection of the flesh.*

Brief reference to the three articles contained in the creed will highlight inconsistency. Examining the first article, 'I believe in God the Father almighty,' scripture reveals that there is no justification for the use of the terminology. The New Testament contains the expressions 'God almighty' and 'God the Father.' The formulation of the first article was inevitable as it was influenced by the baptismal formula.

The second article was extremely controversial. The inversion of Jesus Christ relates to the Old Testament, namely, the Anointed and the Messianic association implicit in Judaism. **St Cyril of Jerusalem** suggested in his *Catecheism,* 'He bears two names, Jesus because he bestows salvation, and Christ because of his priesthood.'

Added to Christ Jesus are two more concepts—the only Son and our Lord. This unique relation to God, 'His only Son,' can be compared with Isaac who was Abraham's 'only son.' Why God preferred a son rather than a daughter was overlooked and raises the question of sex discrimination. Finally, 'Our Lord' implies that the Old Roman creed contains the belief in the pre-existence of Christ Jesus who became incarnate and also belief in virgin birth.

The acceptance of Jesus Christ as God was fundamental in Christian theology. The confession that Jesus was the Son of God was undoubtedly blind faith, so Jesus became the only human being who was not a sinner. This was contradicted by Jesus himself. St Matthew 19 16 & 17 provides the evidence. 'And behold, one came and said unto him, Good Master, what good thing shall I do, that I may have eternal life?

Jesus said unto him, Why callest thou me good? There is none good but one, that is GOD.'

This second article implicit in the Holy Trinity caused upheaval, commonly referred to as the Arian controversy.

The third article refers to the birth and death of Jesus Christ, and his crucifixion and resurrection. The place, 'sits at the right hand of God,' is associated with a similar statement found in Psalm 110 1, 'The Lord said unto my Lord, Sit thou at my right hand.'

The Holy Spirit is a power of God although it was conceived as a divine being, independent of Father and the Son. How it is possible to conceive the Person of the Holy Spirit still remains a mystery, yet it was the spirit that filled the church according to **St Irenaeus,** 'For where the Church is, there is the spirit of God.'

History records that the beginning of the Roman State Church is connected with Emperor Constantine. In 306 AD, after his father's death, the army at once accepted Constantine as their ruler. In 312 AD, after a fierce battle near Rome against his enemy Maxentius, he was converted to Christian faith.

Before and after his conversion, a bitter controversy existed between the Greek and Latin speaking bishops about the second article in the Old Roman creed. An Alexandrian priest, called **Arius** led the opposition against the second article, 'I believe in Christ Jesus, His only Son, our Lord.' The dispute centred on whether Christ was the Son or the Word of God. Obviously, **Arius** was influenced by the opening statement in the Gospel of St John, 'In the beginning was the Word, and the Word was with God, and the Word was God…And the

Word was made flesh.' In a letter to the Bishop of Alexandria, **Arius** wrote, 'Moreover, if another being were to share the divine nature of God in any valid sense, there would be a plurality of divine beings, whereas God by definition is unique.'

There is no doubt, **Arius** believed that Christ Jesus was subordinate to God, therefore, the creed was rejected on the grounds that only the Father was the 'true God.' **Arius** contended that the emergence of the Son depended on the Father's sovereign will and not on God's desire to become flesh.

Constantine was appalled by the state of affairs and in 325 AD. He called a synod of bishops to end the strife between Egypt and Rome. This synod was convened at Nicaea located in the eastern domain of the empire. The 'ecumenical' council discussed the Arian claim, but some bishops inclined to the worship of Christ as 'God incarnate.' When the bishops attempted to draw up their own creed consistent with scriptural language, they found the task impossible. **St Athanasius** realised that a creed was only possible by inserting a new, unambiguous clause but without scriptural authority. The significant clause was, 'From the substance of the Father and of the substance of the Father,' the root of the Trinity doctrine. The Creed of Nicaea was repugnant to **Arius** and **Euzoius** who submitted to **Constantine** in 327 AD a revised creed.

We believe in one God, the Father Almighty; And in the Lord Jesus Christ, His Son, the God-Logos Who was begotten from Him before all ages, through Whom all things came into being, things in heaven and things on earth, Who came down and took flesh and suffered and rose again, ascended to heaven, and will come again to judge living and dead; And in the Holy Spirit, and in the resurrection of the flesh, and in the life of the coming age, and in the kingdom of heaven, and in one Catholic Church of God from end to end of the earth.

Constantine's hope of achieving unity in the Church through the 'ecumenical' council was not realised. A bitter struggle continued until a Dedication Council was set up at Antioch in 341 AD to examine four traditional creeds. No progress was made and the church remained divided. In 381 AD, the second general council agreed to accept the Niceno-Constantinopolitan Creed and it was publicly acclaimed at the Council of Chalcedon in 451 AD. Why there was a 70-years delay before its acceptance has not been discovered. The translation of the Creed follows as made by GL Dossetti (*le simbolo di Nicea e di Constantinopoli*)

We believe in one God, the Father almighty, maker of heaven and earth, of all things visible and invisible; And in one Lord Jesus Christ, the only begotten Son of God, begotten from the Father before all ages, light from light, true God from true God, begotten not made, of one substance with the Father, through whom all things came into existence, Who because of us men and because of our salvation came down from heaven, and incarnate from the Holy Spirit and the Virgin Mary and became man, and was crucified for us under Pontius Pilate, and suffered and was buried, and rose again on the third day according to the Scriptures and ascended to Heaven, and sits on the right hand of the Father, and will come again with glory to judge living and dead, of Whose kingdom there will be no end, And in the Holy Spirit, the Lord and life-giver, Who proceeds from the Father, Who with the Father and the Son is together worshipped and together glorified, Who spoke through the prophets; in one holy Catholic and apostolic Church, We confess one baptism to the remission of sins; we look forward to the resurrection of the dead and the life of the world to come Amen.

The doctrine was seen as the dissolution of Arianism as well as confirmation of the Holy Trinity. It must be emphasised that at the Council of Chalcedon it was confirmed that Jesus Christ existed in two natures—one human and one divine. Theological doctrine has interfered with the unity of the Catholic Church and the cause can be traced to the Holy Trinity.

St Augustine was one of the four Doctors of the Catholic Church. Although he is associated with Neo-Platonism, he never shared the Greek conviction that 'out of nothing, nothing comes,' and he claimed that 'Time' was invented when the universe was created, but God is not part of the irreversible journey. Why? Because God is eternal, there is no alpha and omega and the human conception of 'Time' is subjective.

Augustine believed that truth is the means for a human being to acquire the condition of happiness. He wrote, 'All human beings desire happiness.' When their need and desire is unsatisfied, they are unhappy. Also, most who satisfy their need and desire are not really happy. The key to human happiness is related to what human beings need and desire.

The object of desire ought not to be something temporary, but something of a permanent nature. It must not be limited by chance or fate. An object of decay because of its obedience to the 'Law of Impermanence' cannot satisfy desire permanently. Loving such an object causes unhappiness about its deterioration or loss. Now, since God alone has a permanent nature being eternal and absolutely free, only a human being who desires a relationship with God is able to satisfy the desire for happiness.

Augustine made reason follow in the footsteps of **faith.** The search for truth was summarised in these famous words:

The first step forward…will be to see that the attention is fastened on truth. Of course, faith does not see truth clearly, but it has an eye for it, so to speak, which enables it to see that a thing is true even when it does not see the reason for it. It does not see the thing it believes, but at least it knows for certain that it does not see it, and that it is true none the less. This possession through faith of a hidden but certain truth is the very thing which will impel the mind to penetrate its content, and to elicit the formula, 'Have faith that you may understand' (Credo ut intelligas) explaining its full meaning.

Reasonable faith is a guide for profound conviction.

Anselm submitted the ontological proof for the existence of God (the Greek word *ontos* meaning 'being'). The existence of God is derived from entirely *a priori* premises. The notion of a unique perfect being implies that God must exist. If God did not exist, the notion would not be that of a unique perfect being.

God must exist, otherwise there would be no concept of unique perfection. By referring to the beginning of the 14th Psalm, Anselm attempted to prove to the infidels that they contradict themselves when their hearts do not accept the existence of God. All things by their predicates point to a nature which not only has but is all these predicates.

Like **Augustine**, another Catholic scholar, **Thomas Aquinas** was influenced by a Greek philosopher. In his *Summa contra Gentiles,* he set out his arguments to be used against gentiles who refused to accept the authority of Scripture affirming that the existence of God can be proved.

He asked, 'Firstly, what do we mean by wisdom?' A man is wise when he is aware of the source of blessedness. Now, blessedness is associated with the good of the intellect which is the possession of truth. God possesses the real truth and is the chief object of knowledge, that is, of theology, of science, and their synthesis, philosophy. Direct proofs of reason must be advanced to convince the weak and uneducated of the existence of God. In the proofs for the doctrines of faith, a distinction is required when addressing a believer or an unbeliever. A bare appeal to authority is not enough; reason and philosophy must be the weapons to deter any attacks.

Aquinas dismissed the *ontological* argument submitted by **Anselm**, declaring that no creature has complete knowledge of God's essence, so rejecting any conclusion to be made in support of God's existence. Possibly, **Aquinas** was influenced by **Guanilo** who had rejected **Anselm's** new theology. **Guanilo** argued, the notion of the perfect island, Atlantis, is not adequate proof that it exists. Such a notion is unacceptable. **Aquinas** was then prompted to establish the five proofs of God's existence.

In the *Summa Theologica,* **Aquinas** submitted his first argument which was primarily a reiteration of the 'Unmoved Mover' previously conceived by **Aristotle**. Some objects are only moved by force and others may move or are moved. Movement of an object is related to something that has caused the object to move. There must exist something that moves an object, in other words, there must be a mover. All movement in the universe was produced by the 'Unmoved Mover' who is God. Opponents argue, 'What about rest?'

His second argument for the existence of God which some human beings are most susceptive is the *first cause* argument, although it is often called the *cosmological* argument or the argument from origins. Opponents of the argument question, 'What caused God?' His third argument is related to the 'ultimate cause' argument which is dependent upon God's will. The argument is rejected since volition cannot be considered as an ultimate cause. His fourth argument points to the perfection of harmony and order in the universe which displays the existence of a designer. This popular argument is known as the *teleological* argument or the argument from design. Criticism of the argument relates to the fact that it cannot be the product of benevolent design. Benevolent design insists that life must be possible under all conditions. His final argument is associated with purpose and he refers to inanimate objects supplying a purpose, which involves a being foreign to them, for only animate beings can be involved with purpose. Those who refute the argument question, 'What is the purpose of God's existence?'

After the passing of **Thomas Aquinas**, the Catholic church began to lose its power and reputation due to several factors. The 'Hundred Years' war caused widespread discontent amidst wretched, miserable conditions. Power politics emerged whereby the authority of the Pope was challenged. When the volcano of the **Reformation** finally erupted, the cause can be traced to the corrupt system of religion. **Martin Luther** started the protest movement by nailing his 95 theses to the door of the church in Wittenberg, a place in Germany. It can be seen from these 95 theses that the confrontation with the Roman Catholic Church reduced to three major disagreements.

Luther insisted that all judgements relating to doctrinal and organisation matters must be solely confirmed by scripture and not by church councils and popes. Secondly, **Luther** argued that salvation is the result of justification by faith alone, and it cannot be obtained by absolution from a priest or from works of penance. Similarly, human beings in the role of priest or pope cannot grant forgiveness; **Luther** believed that forgiveness relates to God's grace (sola gratia)

Luther's protest was not really to challenge the supreme authority of the Church of Rome, but to draw attention to the flagrant injustices implicit in the sale of indulgences. For the naive person, an indulgence was a form of protection against retribution by God. **Erasmus** highlighted the exploitation of ignorance, 'Everywhere, the remission of purgatory torment is sold; nor is it sold only, but forced upon those who refuse it.' **Luther** insisted that his 95 theses amounted to a *Disputation for Clarification of the Power of Indulgences.*

As **Luther** firmly believed that all considerations of doctrine must be confirmed by Scripture alone *(sola scriptura)*, he was compelled to reject the existing Catholic creed and preferred the 'Apostles Creed' which is very similar to the 'Old Roman Creed.' The text is copied from the 'Apostles Creed' by HB Swete (London 1894):

I believe in God the Father almighty, creator of heaven and earth; And in Jesus Christ, His only Son, our Lord, Who was conceived by the Holy Spirit, born from the Virgin Mary, suffered under Pontius Pilate, was crucified, dead and buried, descended to hell, on the third day rose again from the dead, ascended to heaven, sits on the right hand of God the Father almighty, thence he will come to judge the living and the dead; I believe in the Holy

Spirit, the holy Catholic Church, the communion of saints, the remission of
sins, the resurrection of the flesh, and eternal life.   *Amen.*

Martin Luther substituted Christian for Catholic, but the Reformation led
only to minimal reform. Rome accepted the revised 'confession of faith' as
Luther had completely ignored D*e Trinitatis erroribus* (Errors of the Trinity).
When analysed, the creed is a summary of the gospels of St Matthew and St
Luke. In the gospels of St Mark and St John, there is no mention of the Virgin
Mary, the assumed 'Mother of God.'

The word 'Trinity' means the combination of three persons or things as one.
The first to use the term was **Theophilus,** Bishop of Antioch 181 AD when
referring to the three days of creation prior to the creation of the sun and moon.
His Holy Trinity consisted of God, God's word and God's wisdom. Also, the
resurrection of the flesh was assumed by St Paul to be the foundation of the
Christian faith. This belief conflicts with the cycle of all forms of life; birth,
growth, decay and death. It is appropriate to quote the text which emanated from
an eminent authority. 'The Three Creeds, Nicene Creed, Athanasius Creed, and
that which is called the Apostles Creed,' ought thoroughly to be received and
believed; for they may be proved by most certain warrants of Holy Scripture—
Articles of Religion, Church of England, Article VIII.

The Reformation achieved one significant result; it gave citizens access to
spiritual nourishment by having the Bible printed in their own language; it also
gave them a craving for liberty. Alas! It never gave them truth, and it paved the
way for Capitalism. It has been pointed out that it was essential for the
Reformation movement to emerge in the sixteenth century, otherwise the church
may not have survived.

Francis Bacon made the division of theology into the Natural and the
Revealed. Knowledge of God from that which can be acquired by the study of
nature is Natural Theology, whereas all other knowledge must come under the
banner of Revealed Theology. By the use of metaphor, his words are paraphrased
as follows: '*Because of the uncharted waters, it is prudent to quit the small raft
of reason and climb aboard the vessel of the church where the divine instrument
is located to correctly chart the course. Our previous guide, the stars of
philosophy are of no further use since we have a duty to obey the divine law,
though the will is reluctant to comply. Likewise, it is common sense to believe in
the Word of God, though our reason is disturbed by it.*'

Thomas Hobbes made the claim that philosophy is entirely concerned with the corporeal as the only kind of existence. He even conceived that God is a corporeal being, yet at the same time, he asserted that God is not an object of knowledge. Denying that theology emerges from reason but arises from supernatural revelation, he thought that it is immediately excluded from philosophy and the intermingling of faith and reason is a sin against both. **Hobbes** believed that God ruled the world through powerful kings who are automatically heads of the church; no human soul could exist in a material universe.

Descartes accepted **Newton's** 'first law of motion' stating that 'everybody continues in its state of rest or of uniform motion in a straight line unless acted upon by an external force.' In his *Meditations*, he alluded to the ontological argument when he wrote, 'the existence of God ought to pass in my mind as being at least as certain as I have up to this time regarded the truths of mathematics to be, which have to do only with numbers and figures.' For **Descartes**, God existed in pure spirit, but the 'first law of motion' assumes there is a mover. Is it possible for pure spirit to act upon matter to give it motion? Arguments and proofs for the existence of God are futile, for they have no significance as verification is impossible.

Blaise Pascal agreed with **Descartes** in that God is pure spirit and maintained that knowledge of God can be obtained only via spiritual experience. It is opportune to refer to **Pascal's** famous wager, paraphrased below.

Let us examine the propositions, 'God exists or God does not exist.' Which side shall we incline? Reason can decide nothing here. According to reason, you cannot defend either of the two options because neither can be proved. If you do not choose, then what good is freedom of choice? It is not a question of like or dislike. It is a question of faith. You have to gamble, you are committed, which option will you take? If you bet on the notion, 'God exists,' and you are right; you win everything. If you are wrong; you lose nothing. If you bet on the notion, 'God does not exist' and you are wrong; what a terrible misfortune that would be! On the other hand, if you are right, then you win an argument.

The destiny of man was outlined by Pascal in his unfinished work called *Les Pensees*.

Who will unravel this mess? Nature refutes the sceptics, and reason refutes the dogmatists. What then will become of you, oh men, who try to discover by your own natural reason, what is your true condition?

Know then, proud man, what a paradox you are unto thyself. Humble thyself weak reason; be silent foolish nature; learn that man infinitely transcends man, and learn from your Master what is your true condition, of which you are ignorant. Hear God.

This recognition that reason cannot help to unravel the mess means that we must depend on faith alone.

Spinoza substituted the dualism, *body/mind* of **Descartes** by a monism where God is the single independent substance of the universe. God is both a concept in the mind and a pebble on the beach. God is all, or God is in all objects.

Leibniz asserted that 'contingency' is a factor in the universe, for there is no reason for it not to exist, but there is no evidence to indicate why it exists. However, **Leibniz** maintained that every part in the universe must have a sufficient reason to exist, therefore the whole of the universe must have sufficient reason to exist. The sufficient reason is external to the universe and exists as God.

John Locke was consistent with his conviction that innate ideas are not possible, so it follows that it is impossible to have an innate idea of God. Is it possible to have an experience of God? **Locke** affirmed that God exists because human beings must have been produced by some omnipotent being. **Locke** conceived God as a spiritual substance and asserted that we have ideas of three kinds of substances only—of God, of finite intelligence and of bodies, so a triad is formed, namely, God, mind and matter.

Bishop Berkeley taught that everything in the universe is always in the hand of God and our knowledge of God depends upon an understanding entirely different from the physical world. We are aware that physical events will conform to certain 'laws of nature' which are related to our convenience and happiness. God is the cause of the natural world and because God is infinite spirit, our world is spiritual not material.

David Hume was an intense sceptic but thought that a belief in the existence of God was essential for any doctrine of morality to be recognised. He argued that God caused the existence of the universe stressing that this cannot be proved by reason. Also, he admitted the possibility that as the soul is related to the body, so may God be related to the world, although no proof is possible. In his *Dialogues Concerning Natural Religion,* **Hume** wrote to some length refuting the arguments for the existence of God. Whilst remaining sceptical about the nature of God, he suggested that we introduce a theology which is necessary to produce a right human attitude.

Immanuel Kant, in his 'Critique of Pure Reason' dismisses the ontological argument by insisting that existence is not a predicate. Referring to the teleological argument, he concedes that the universe reveals a complex order, thereby raising the question of purpose. However, it only proves a designer has been at work and not a creator. The conception of a designer cannot be equated with the conception of God. He was certain that it is impossible to prove that God exists, but the moral life has no foundation without the existence of God.

Obviously, **Kant** had been influenced by **Hume** who asserted that reason does not provide us with any proof that God exists. Similarly, can reason provide us with any proof that God does not exist? Because of the host of invalid arguments about the existence of God, **Kant** introduced the term 'transcendent' as the idea of God, simply because God transcends experience. Of course, this was a cogent response to the empirical philosophers who all subscribed to the view that knowledge is dependent upon sense-experience.

Hegel pointed to the fact that religion appears in different forms. The Hindu religion honours God but degrades man. The religion of Ancient Greece honoured man but degraded God. Then there is the Christian religion in which man and the divine are united, the GOD-MAN, namely, JESUS CHRIST. This is the *logos* which **Plato** and **Aristotle** discussed, and which St John referred to in the first sentence of his gospel. Therefore, for **Hegel**, Christianity is the absolute religion and the dialectical process taking place in evolution is a process appertaining to God's plan.

Karl Marx was firmly convinced that God does not exist. He was prompted to change the history of the chosen race to the history of the chosen class as he believed that all history is really a history of the class struggle. He declared that religion is the opium for the masses whereby they are drugged into the acceptance of capitalist-bourgeois beliefs. **Marx** perceived that religious beliefs have been an asset to particular institutions, who have exploited the ignorance of the masses for certain classes to retain political power and social privileges. Fact is stranger than fiction; **Marx** was born a Jew, then baptised a Christian before becoming an atheist.

Francis Bradley is regarded as the leading British idealist. He presented a theological puzzle that defies a satisfactory answer. If the Absolute is associated with the TOTALITY of BEING, then it results in pure *pantheism,* so that whatever occurs in the universe, it must be associated with the WILL of GOD, whether it is good or evil. However, Christian theology affirms that God has willed to create and preserve free spirit in BEING, so there is at least relative independence, yet the actions of human beings may be and frequently are in direct contradiction to the Will of God. Therefore, this must reveal a limitation with respect to the absoluteness of God. **Bradley** maintained that knowledge of the Absolute is obtainable and it is the only subject of predicates.

Soren Kierkegaard is known as the first *existentialist* and existentialism is really a philosophy of life. He claimed that human beings are unable to obtain certain knowledge and in recognising this fact, the way to escape from this undesirable situation is via faith alone; faith in the possibility of having a relationship with God. Significantly, **Kierkegaard** observed that human beings are alienated from the natural world by their materialistic philosophy, and alienated from God by their naive humanism. He thought that we are 'displaced persons' living in a world where truth is solely subjective.

Friedrich Nietzche claimed that **Darwin** had destroyed any belief in God and in his book, 'Thus Spake Zarathustra,' he displayed a scorn of the female sex and a repugnance of Christianity. He stated that women are incapable of friendship, they are still cats, or birds, or at best cows, so that childbirth is their only useful purpose for the production of warriors. He was contemptuous of the mob's stupidity in accepting the 'slave morality' which depended upon submission to the Christian God. In a world where 'God is dead' and everything is permitted, his 'master morality' reduces to *moil* or nothing; no values, no God and no purpose of life.

William James was consistent with his *pragmatism* when in his 'The Will to Believe,' he insists that human beings are sometimes prompted to take decisions on matters where there is no information to aid the decision-making. A religious decision is the classic case as there is neither proof about God's existence nor any proof about the nature of God. Therefore, the Will to Believe is a precondition for a belief in God, which is more or less a basic need to develop the nature of a human being.

It would be an act of sheer prejudice not to refer to other major religions. Apart from tribal religions, **Judaism** is the most ancient religion. Other religions have made use of the Hebrew scriptures, especially the 'Law Covenant' given by God to the Jewish people via the mediator **Moses.** The chosen race was ordered to reject *idolatry* as expressed in the second of the 'Ten Commandments.' The last six commandments showed the way that God wished human beings to behave. Although the Old Testament is the root of Judaism containing written law, prophecies and poetical works, the essential fertiliser is the **Talmud,** which is a written explanation of the oral law given to Moses on Mount Sinai. This oral law was established in writing by the moral leaders called **rabbis.**

Like Christianity, modern Judaism has been influenced by Greek philosophy. The resurrection of the body is no longer considered as one of the central doctrines of Judaism; it is accepted that a human being has an immortal soul that survives death. The Catholic creeds have been a significant factor in the rejection of Jesus Christ; the doctrine of the 'Trinity' is regarded as blasphemous and inconsistent with scripture: 'The Lord our God, THE LORD IS ONE.'

The next religion to be considered is one that appears to have more magnetism than the Christian religion, namely, **ISLAM.** The word has a special meaning for Muslims as it involves 'surrender' or 'submission' to the Arabic God or ALLAH. The Muslim holy book is called the 'KORAN' which equates to 'Recitation.' **Muhammad** received a command from the angel, Gabriel, to become a prophet and he received a series of revelations which are the inspired words written in the 'Koran.' The faith of Muhammad was rejected by his own tribe, forcing him to flee from Mecca, the place where he was born. Eventually, he returned to Mecca to become its ruler; he took revenge by declaring war on all infidels and threw out the idolatrous images from the Ka'bah.

In the 'Koran,' there is criticism of the Jews for breaking their Covenant and also relating to the 'Trinity' doctrine; the raising of Jesus to equality with God. In chapter 4:171, this advice is given, 'Desist Trinity doctrine; it will be better for you: for God is One God.' The 'Koran' affirms that God receives the souls of human beings at the time of their death, and also refers to the 'Rising of the Dead.' Is it to be assumed that God requires 'body and soul?'

Buddhism is not so much a religion but more a spiritual philosophy. The principal purpose of Buddhism is to achieve 'Enlightenment' for oneself, and to show brotherly love to all men without distinction, and to behave kindly to all members of the animal kingdom. To the Buddhist, everything relates to the mind which stands aloof from circumstances; 'Our character is the result of our thoughts; it is founded on our thoughts, made up of our thoughts.' A brief summary of Buddhism has been reduced to twelve principles, extracted are the main tenets to achieve 'Enlightenment,' which are derived not from God, but from the recognition of four Noble Truths and knowledge of the Noble Eight-fold Path of self-development.

The first fact of existence is the 'law of change or impermanence.'

All forms of life pass through the same cycle of existence, that is, birth, growth, decay and death. No one owns the life that flows in him or her any more than an electric light bulb owns the current that gives it light.

Karma, meaning action-reaction which relates to cause and effect governs all existence.

Life being One, the interests of the part should be those of the whole. In his ignorance, man thinks he can successfully strive for his own interests, but his selfishness produces suffering. The Buddha taught four noble truths.

(i)   The miseries of human existence.
(ii) The origin of misery is desire, or the craving for success.
(iii) Destruction of desire leads to freedom from misery.
(iv) The way which leads to the destruction of desire is via the noble eight-fold path.

The eight-fold path implicates; Right Views or preliminary under- standing, Right Aims or Motive, Right Speech, Right Behaviour, Right Livelihood. Right Effort, Right Concentration or mind development, and finally, *Samadhi,* (Right Contemplation).

As Buddhism is a way of living, not merely a theory of life, the treading of the path is essential for spiritual development. The essence of Buddhism is summed up by the Buddha himself:

> *Cease to do evil,*
> *Strive to do good,*
> *Purify thy heart.*

Nirvana is obtained when there is complete freedom from all desire; it is really impossible to conceive, it can only be experienced. A finite mind can have no cognition of the infinite. The Buddha said, 'Work out your own salvation with diligence.' Buddhism does not deny the existence of God or soul though it has its own meaning with respect to these concepts. Buddhism is a training of the mind, a form of religion, a spiritual guidance and a way of life.

To define **Hinduism** is not simple; there is simultaneously, a belief in one God as well as many Gods and Goddesses. This polytheism accepts that there is one supreme God and all other Gods are subordinate to the one. However, there are favourite Gods that form a trinity—*Brahma* is the Creator; *Vishnu* is the Preserver, and *Siva* is the Destroyer.

Hindu teaching affirms the belief in the immortality of the soul and the ancient writings are the VEDAS which have been supplemented by the *Brahmanas* and the *Upanishads.* The *Brahmanas* describe how sacrifices and rituals are to be accomplished; the *Upanishads,* alternatively called *Vedanta* are writings explaining the cause of all thought and action relating to Hindu philosophy. Central to this philosophy is **Karma** which involves the belief that every action has its consequences, which affects the future life of the transmigrated soul. Free Will is non-existent in Hinduism; man is considered as a mere seed in the field of fate.

It is not certain whether **Confucianism** and **Taoism** are religions. The word 'Tao' means the way; it is the way all men ought to tread in imitation of the harmony and orderliness in the universe. **CS Lewis** in his book described the 'Tao' thus: 'It is the doctrine of objective value, the belief that certain attitudes are really true, and others really false, to the kind of thing the universe is and the kind of things we are.' **Lao-tzu** believed 'All things arise from the Tao…They are nourished by virtue, formed from matter and shaped by environment.'

Charles Darwin was the founder of a doctrine which has had a powerful influence on human thought. For over a hundred years, it has been accepted as a science; it is paradoxical that 'chance' or 'thought exclusion' has brainwashed human beings into believing that there is no supreme intelligence behind the universe. Scant theories with respect to big bangs, black holes, little universes, have all been submitted as possible scenarios appertaining to the origin of what exists. Of course, metaphysics was eliminated and replaced by 'scientific method.' However, it can now be observed that metaphysics was not eliminated, it was replaced by false metaphysics.

Poetic justice has begun to emerge; many scientists have used the exceptional factor in their level of being, namely, their reasoning ability to present a metaphysical argument that puts God back into the physical world. Science eliminated God from the physical world and the scientist's ethical relativism was an attempt to eliminate God from the moral world. Scientists were so certain in rowing in with the 'evolution doctrine' and never considered the possibility of losing their oars.

The 'Anthropic Principle' has made an exception to the 'uncertainty principle;' it now emerges that the study of 'being' is now a serious activity. It has been realised that after the Big Bang, laws of nature had to conform to such perfect precision to create a universe in which human life and intelligence could exist; it could not have been the result of a cosmic accident. It is now acknowledged that the balance of essential diverse quantities and forces in the universe, from the sub-atomic to other celestial bodies, is in such fine mathematical precision, it is impossible to dispute that there was a plan. The 'Anthropic Principle' resurrects the belief that there is a divine being behind the universe. God never died; God was merely forgotten.

The church which has been on the defensive for so long is now presented with an opportunity to convert many sceptics. Unfortunately, it will not be possible to seize the opportunity if it continues to subscribe to 'Trinity' doctrine, belief in virgin birth and resurrection of the body. The Protestant movement was not really a challenge to the authority of the Church of Rome, but to draw attention to the pressure selling of papal indulgences.

To make Christianity more acceptable, there must be some form of **Regeneration** within the church. The duty of the church is to emphasise that ultimately, Christianity is a life to be lived rather than a theological system to be accepted. Further, the leaders of the church must heed the words of Jesus, especially in St Matthew 21 and 'practise what they preach.'

On Wednesday, 17 January 1996, at Coventry Cathedral, a service was held to commemorate the centenary of the motor car. At the start, an 1897 Daimler Autocar was driven up the aisle, and the bishop claimed that it represented the thanksgiving for all the benefits the motor car had bestowed. A modern Lady Godiva appeared on the scene aiming to stop the service; she protested that the motor car had been a curse to mankind. It is appropriate to quote from St John 2: 13 to 16.

Jesus went up to Jerusalem, and found in the temple those that sold oxen, sheep and doves, and the changers of money sitting; And when he had made a scourge of small cords, he drove them all out of the temple, and the sheep,

and the oxen; and poured out the changers' money, and overthrew the tables;
And said unto them, Take these things hence; make not my Father's house a
house of merchandise.

There can be no other conclusion than that Jesus was an angry man which showed that he was a mortal man, but he was also a divine messenger. Western man, before **Socrates**, recognised the inherent dualism of his nature-rational and savage. **Dante** expressed the fundamental belief on which western civilisation has been established.

Man has been endowed with a threefold life, namely, vegetable, animal and rational. He journeys along a threefold road; for in so as he is vegetable, he seeks for what is useful, wherein he is of like nature as the plants; in so far as he is animal, he seeks for that which gives him pleasure, wherein he is of like nature as the brutes; in so far as he is rational, he seeks for what is right—and in this, he stands alone, or imitates the nature of divine being.

Chapter 5
Ethics and Egoism

It is apt to refer to the great poetical works of Dante, his 'Divine Comedy.' The pilgrim, Dante, sets out on his journey of three stages: first, the descent into the *Inferno,* the 'savage place' from which Virgil, representing art, helps him to escape and then he had to endurethe process of *Purgatory* in which Beatrice, representing religion helps him intervene for his salvation and helps him to climb the mountain to reach the Garden of Eden; the beginning of the third stage, the vision of *Paradise, so different from the first stage.* The following extracts are relevant to previous chapters.

For when our intellect is drawing close
To its desire, its path is so profound
That memory cannot follow where it goes.

What faith holds here shall be known by seeing,
Not demonstrated, but self-evident
Like those prime truths that brook no disagreeing.

Yet, since on earth your schoolmen argue still
Those mid endowments of angelic nature
Are understanding, memory and will;

I'll tell thee more, that purged of all conjecture,
The truth thou wilt see, of which men speak amiss.
Confounding here two senses when they lecture.

Ye on the earth, in your philosophy,
Are not for long content to tread one path,
Enamoured of vain show and subtlety.

Dante strongly criticised the adversaries of justice, especially the church and with their temperance ambition, thus betraying their spiritual beliefs.

Like Dante in the 'Divine Comedy,' society has descended into the 'Inferno' to experience the real nature of sin and corruption. **Dorothy L Sayers** made the following perception of society in her 'Introductory Papers on Dante.'

T*he Inferno* is a picture of society in a state of sin and corruption, that most will readily agree. And since we are today well convinced that society is in a bad way, we find it easy enough to recognise the stages by which the depth of corruption has reached. Futility; lack of a living faith; the drift into loose morality; greedy consumption; financial irresponsibility; uncontrolled bad temper; a self-opinionated and obstinate individualism; violence, lack of reverence for life and property, the exploitation of sex, the debasing of language by advertisement and propaganda, the commercialising of religion, and the pandering to superstition; the conditioning of people's minds by mass-hysteria and 'spell-binding' of all kinds, bribery and string pulling in public affairs, hypocrisy, dishonesty in material things, intellectual dishonesty…the falsification and exploitation of all the means of communication;…these are the all-too-recognisable stages that lead to the instability of society and the breakdown of all civilised relations.

Surprising as it may appear, these Papers were presented in 1957. Although **Dorothy Sayers's** perception of society was rejected as mere pessimism over sixty years ago, only those wearing rose-tinted spectacles would reject it today. What a host of bad habits that were recognised.

A nation without God's guidance is a nation without order. Proverbs 29:18

There is a current inclination to equate knowledge with many of the hypotheses of science. However, science can only provide the means, it cannot provide us with the knowledge relating to how those means ought to be used. It may well be, in the long term, science has caused problems that it is unable to solve, such as the storage of the long-existence radioactive wastes, for unlike other pollutants, there is no way of destroying radioactivity. **Therefore,** the argument cannot be refuted; scientific studies ought to include the study of the right way to use the information acquired from its methods. If we have any tendency to be moral beings, then we must all be interested in this subject. Profound thinkers of the past have specialised in this subject, primarily by intuition.

Sadly, the image of scientists has been damaged by some in their profession falsifying the results from their research. In 1987, in the periodical 'Nature,' it was asserted that 'scientific fraud and carelessness among researchers could be widespread.' Without a shadow of doubt, 'fraud in science' exists, but the question arises, 'Can fraud in ethics exist?' Intuition informs us that 'fraud in science' is wrong, but 'fraud in ethics' tends to obey the 'law of contradiction.' Inevitably, ethics involves both moral thinking as well as moral action. In relation to ethics, a significant question is asked, 'Why should we do what is right?' The simple answer is that we benefit by doing what is right.

In *etymology,* the Greek word 'ethical' is equivalent to the Latin word 'moral.' These two words relate to 'habits,' although 'Ethics' is an enquiry into how human beings ought to act in general circumstances; always to treat another human being as an end and never as a means. The pair of polar concepts right/wrong, good/bad, need to be highlighted; right/wrong are primarily adjectives of action whereas good/bad may describe a situation or behaviour, a character or a person. Theories which consider right/wrong as the primary concepts are called *deontological* theories, insisting that 'duty is prior to value,' but some of our duties are independent of value, such as 'promise-keeping.' Theories which consider good/bad as the primary concepts are called *teleological* theories; virtue or moral excellence entails the value, goodness. Theories which consider the good-in-itself or the valuable as the primary concept, so leading to value judgements are called *axiological ethics.*

Protagoras, in declaring, 'Man is the measure of all things,' dismissed any universal standard of human action, as every human being can measure what is right and what is wrong. The inevitable consequence is that 'anarchy must reign.' Hence, the Sophists indirectly goaded human reason to prove that moral laws exist.

Socrates challenged the Sophists; how can a man measure virtue when 'virtue is knowledge.' He maintained that the awareness of ignorance is a precondition for the acquisition of knowledge. This is the first step in the quest for knowledge, but when **Socrates** questioned the Sophists what certain words meant, he received no satisfactory answers from them. Without the concepts of wisdom, justice and goodness; a person cannot talk about acting wisely, justly or in good faith. If a person uses the same words but attaches a different meaning to them, then a communication breakdown occurs, and when the words relate to ethics, then there is a moral disagreement. This dual problem relating to truth and moral behaviour prompted **Socrates** to claim, 'virtue is knowledge.'

Socrates was the first to identify the 'principle of conscience,' which has been defined as a subjective sensibility embracing objective content. For **Socrates**, conscience is the God or *daemon* that speaks from the heart which is the property of every human being. He firmly believed that no man does wrong willingly; he does wrong simply because he lacks knowledge. **Socrates** perceived that true wisdom is associated with the fulfilment of the Delphic instruction, 'Know thyself,' for to be critical of another human being's conduct and simultaneously to be ignorant of thine own behaviour is nothing short of stupidity.

In existing society, many think that 'ethics' is not a practical subject, it is purely theoretical. The question is—why is 'ethics' assumed to be purely theoretical? This false assumption can be eliminated by examining the result of an inquiry conducted by **Plato.** He discovered that although there were many teachers specialising in mathematics, medicine and building science, there were very few teachers specialising in the subject of goodness or virtue. Moral philosophers have fastened on to this paradox. It is important that any person who wishes to become a mathematician, a doctor or a civil engineer, should learn to become a good mathematician, a good doctor or a good civil engineer. Then it cannot be denied that a human being should learn to become a good human being. The practical questions relating to society arise. Is it better to be a good human being or a bad human being? What is good human behaviour? What is a right action? Am I responsible for my actions? Can it be denied that these questions have practical implications?

Plato claimed that goodness is independent of human opinion and desires. Goodness is similar to a mathematical equation and is considered to be an absolute. An absolute is something that requires no justification. **Plato** was the first great opponent to 'Situation Ethics' which is a private code of morality. He foresaw the emergence of this destructive code and countered it by considering the nature of reality. He claimed that human beings live in two worlds; the world of the senses which is dominated by the appetites, and the world of the intellect which is dominated by reason. The former is an unreal world whereas the latter is the real world; in other words, the world of ideas. For **Plato**, the ideas are ends which are all subordinated to the highest end as their principle; the Good, or the idea of the Good, is constantly portrayed by him as the idea of all ideas or the absolute idea.

Like **Socrates**, **Plato** rejected the philosophical doctrine of *hedonism*, for to equate goodness with pleasure means the maximum pursuit of pleasure is justified irrespective of the harm inflicted upon others. An unreflective pursuit of pleasure frequently causes pain. Identified with the pleasure attraction are two persuasive forces in the mind, the force of reason and the force of desire. When human beings are presented with the conflict of reason and desire, many side with desire. Reason needs an ally to conquer desire and *thymos* forms a special relationship with reason. This partner is described as the stead-fast spirit of a human being or more commonly known as 'strength of will.' *Eros* is usually associated with one aspect of passion, but **Plato** conceived it to mean the unrestricted desire for goodness and happiness. In the 'Symposium,' Diotima reveals the change from *Eros;* the change from the love in one world to the love in an alternative world. In this transformation from the desire for goodness via *Eros,* we enter into the aesthetic world. The two world doctrine of **Plato** is not conceivable to those whose beliefs are limited to the material world.

Diotima informed **Socrates** that the comprehension of beauty is like climbing a mystical mountain. The first stage involves a separation from physical beauty; the next stage is to struggle to a point where moral beauty leaves the climber breathless with approval; the next stage is to reach the height where the beauty of knowledge contained in a mathematical formula or a scientific law urges the climber to continue the struggle to reach the summit; at this stage, the climber has escaped from the world of material things to the world of intelligible things. Finally, in reaching the summit, the climber encounters beauty itself, and discovers the secret of absolute beauty. Diotima emphasised, 'This above all others is the region where a man's life should be spent, in the contemplation of absolute beauty…Do you not see in that region alone where he perceives beauty with the faculty capable of perceiving it, he will be able to bring forth not mere reflected images of goodness, but true goodness, because he will not be in contact with a reflection but the truth? And having brought forward and nurtured true goodness he will have the privilege of being beloved by God and becoming immortal himself.'

Aristotle noticed that the subjective experience relating to what is thought as 'good,' forms a precondition of its proper understanding. First, an answer must be given to the question. 'What is the highest good attainable by action?' Aristotle answered with one word, 'Happiness,' and so investigated what activity leads to this condition. This activity implicates a rational being rather than an irrational being. In a rational being, there are two classes of virtue, logical and moral, agreeing with the two parts of the soul. Logical virtues are acquired by the way of instruction whereas moral virtues are acquired by the way of habit. It is the responsibility of the government to mould a citizen's character to be good by developing good habits. Citizens acquire a sense of justice by acting justly. Eventually, Aristotle arrived at the following definition, 'Happiness is an activity of the soul in accord with perfect virtue.'

Aristotle referred to the choice of rational beings as opposed to irrational beings. The choice is the 'Golden Mean;' for example; temperance is a mean between excess and denial; justice is a mean between mercy and cruelty. Therefore, a rational being is one who uses the 'Golden Mean' which is determined by reason, thereby avoiding extremes of action. Aristotle expressed it as follows:

Virtue is a state of character derived from settled habits, involving deliberate choice, resting in a 'mean' that is relative to ourselves, the 'mean' subject to determination by a rational principle, and in the way in which the man of practical wisdom would determine it. Aristotle's 'Golden Mean' is a philosophy of temperance which cannot be accepted as there is no 'Golden Mean' between telling the truth and not telling the truth. Plato and Aristotle both hoped that the 'good life' would be pursued as a result of their philosophical doctrines. The Epicureans claimed that the 'good life' consisted solely in *hedonistic* activity, or that pleasure is the highest good. The philosophy of Epicurus was narrowly confined to how pleasure can be gained and pain avoided. He made a distinction between passive and active pleasures. Passive pleasures are more preferable since they are free from painful experience. Greater activity of the mind is better than over-exertion of the body, therefore pleasures of the intellectual life satisfy much more. Active pleasures unrestrained tend to unbalance the body, thus causing pain, like the excessive consumption of alcohol will cause headache or nausea. It appears the absence of pain is preferable to the occurrence of pleasure. Epicurus thought that pleasure is obtained either by the satisfaction of desire or by the restriction of desire. The complete satisfaction of a desire means that it no longer exists. The Stoics asserted that the 'good life' can only be obtained if man acts in harmony with the universe. However, it is not necessary for man to know nature generally, but only his own nature. Thus, from the maxim that man should act in harmony with reason, there is a gradual transition to the belief that man should act harmoniously. From the study of human nature alone, there arises the conception of 'duty,' until then unknown in Greek philosophy. The Stoics advised an attitude of indifference to worldly affairs, stressing that man becomes a philosopher by giving importance only to that which is independent of all external circumstances and entirely dependent upon himself.

Epictetus was convinced that virtue lies in the 'will;' it is only the 'will' that makes a man good or bad. Freedom from passion and disturbance is a prerequisite for happiness and such a freedom means that we should love our enemies. To live in harmony with the universe and to live in harmony with thine own species, this is the philosophy the Stoics presented. Can this suspicion be justified? Did Jesus Christ derive his two great commandments from Stoic philosophy?

Early Christian thinkers returned to the Old Testament which recorded that man was made in God's image, pure and good, but he was tempted away from God by the desire for the forbidden fruit, instead of the desire for a relationship with God, so sin came into existence. This original sin by man which is described symbolically in Genesis was spread like the plague to all men, and the only way to escape from the disease that is identified as evil, is through the divine Grace of God. This account is consistent with the dualism present in most religions, namely, material experiences tend to attract evil and spiritual experiences attract the good.

Augustine argued that since the name philosopher denotes a friend of wisdom, and God is wisdom, hence, the philosopher is a lover of God. Scripture commands us to flee, not from philosophy, but only from that of this world. Whatever leads to the knowledge of God has value; and therefore 'physics' is justifiable. God is great without quantity, good without quality, without space present and without time eternal. **Augustine** attempted to answer the pertinent question, 'How could God create a universe in which evil abounds?'

Augustine indicated that the proper core of the spiritual character is formed by the will of man. In reality, the conduct of man is like the necessary fruit of a good or bad tree. The man who wills of himself and wills his own will is evil, he is a slave. Only divine grace makes man free and whoever becomes free depends solely on God. Therefore, the inability to do good is related to all of those whom God does not make free from sin. In his book, *City of God*, **Augustine** introduces two cities; the heavenly city shall reign eternally with God and the earthly city is ruled by the devil. In one chapter, he expressed his passionate opposition to judicial torture, but simultaneously justifies the 'theory of the just **war.'**

Early Christian thinkers approved the policy of 'pacifism,' since the New Testament explicitly opposes any form of military conflict. Is it possible simultaneously to love and kill your enemy? **Augustine** was prompted to borrow the pagan notion of *justum bellum* to devise his 'theory of the just war,' in which the harmful action of a man is of no importance providing the heart is pure. He dogmatised, 'All soldiering is instituted either to repel injury or to inflict punishment—injury is repelled either by one's own person or from one's associates—and both things are prohibited by the law of the gospels. Christ's 'precepts of patience' do not suggest that war is evil, for those precepts are addressed rather to the preparation of the heart, which is internal, than to the deed which takes place publicly. The evil of war resides in the mind; the soldier which thrusts his sword into the enemy is motivated by benevolence and pity, thereby acting in accordance with the teaching of Jesus Christ.' Most certainly, **Augustine's** scriptural interpretation may be challenged about its validity. When attempting to reconcile his 'theory of the just war' with his belief that a relationship with God is attained via a love of God and not via love of the earthly city, the conclusion that **Augustine** acted like King Lear cannot be denied.

Thomas Aquinas insisted that the ultimate end after which everything strives is the ground of all things, God; and in the universal struggle to become a similar nature, there is produced a series of steps, in which each is the goal of the preceding one. Happiness is not gained from pleasure, wealth or power, and it is not related to the senses; it is gained by the contemplation of God. Love to God and to one's neighbour forms the essential content of law. Evil emerges from secondary causes, namely, the goodness or badness resulting from a particular action depends upon the purpose of the actor. **Aquinas** disagreed with **Augustine** that it depended upon an actor's intention; an evil act may become a good act. Intention cannot change an evil act into a good act, but intention is necessary to cause an act to be undeniably good. Evil is destitute of goodness, yet all things created by God strive for goodness, evil results from a failure to strive sufficiently.

Christian ethics which primarily involve the teachings of Jesus Christ gradually became absorbed into church ethics. During this period of absorption, theological arguments occurred incessantly. From the practice of identifying the Virgin Mary as the 'Mother of God,' such a belief caused fierce arguments. **Charles Gore** in his excellent work, 'Philosophy of the Good Life,' stresses that Christianity is a life to be lived rather than a theology to be accepted.

A central feature of Christian ethics is related to the Old Testament, namely, the Decalogue, or more commonly known as the Ten Commandments, it is strange that the Decalogue does not mention truth yet Pontius Pilate questioned, 'What is truth?' To eliminate any false impression, the Ten Commandments are a set of laws that are unique in the whole of human history, and they are an indispensable guide for the good life. Now, when a person breaks a commandment, a sin is committed. The notion of sin is related to an archer 'missing the mark' of perfect obedience, or employing the modern concept; sin is a failure to obey a moral principle.

If you were to ask the average person in the street to name two of the 'seven deadly sins,' it is short odds that you would receive a negative response and possibly be ridiculed. There seems to be a consensus of opinion that sin is old-fashioned, yet there is public concern about the type and frequency of crime. Politicians experience no difficulty in making speeches on the subject of crime, but most tend to be embarrassed when the subject is sin. Many escape from their embarrassment by pointing to the fact that they sit in the House of Parliament, not in the House of God. The significant question is raised, 'What is the difference between a crime and a sin?'

Strangely, no legal definition of a crime exists. However, it is generally accepted that a crime is a wrongful act against the State and punishable by the State. How is a wrongful act recognised? It is recognised when an individual breaks a law. What is the meaning of 'law?' There are two interpretations:

(a) in the universal sense, a law is a rule to which actions conform or should conform; (b) in the rigid sense, a law is a rule of behaviour imposed by a State upon its citizens and enforced by the courts. Interest intensifies when it is recalled that a sin is a wrongful act against God. Both a sin and a crime are wrongful acts but a sin is related to the rules of morality. So, what is the difference between the rules of law and the rules of morality? There is no difference except in their method of enforcement.

Let us consider a specific crime. In the Decalogue, the Sixth Commandment states, 'Thou shalt not kill' (another human being). In criminal law, **'murder'** means 'unlawfully killing a reasonable creature in being and under the Queen's peace, with malice aforethought, the death following within a year and a day.' In earlier times, murder was classified as a felony but the modern classification substitutes 'indictable offence' for this serious crime. It is appropriate to show the distinction between the Decalogue and criminal law (man-made law). Recent historical events have shown the futility and irrationality of war and its evil effects. First, the allied bombing of an air raid shelter in Baghdad, killing women and children; second, the bombing of two refugee convoys and the Chinese Embassy in Belgrade. The irony is that a war crimes tribunal has been set up to consider the actions of some Bosnian Serb leaders. Roland wrote, 'O liberty! How many crimes are committed in thy name?'

Specifically, in criminal law, 'malice aforethought' means previously thought that death would or might result. Without fear of contradiction, according to the Decalogue, the allied action in Iraq was evil and lest it may be misconstrued, Saddam Hussein's evil actions are recorded. To forestall any criticism of self-righteousness, all men have sinned including 'yours truly.' Although confession is good for the individual soul, it is the mending of foolish ways that is to be desired. However, in criminal law, the allied action in Iraq was not a crime although thousands of human beings were killed. Indeed, celebrations in the form of parades were organised to applaud the efficiency of the mass-murder operation and here lies the rub. In an education system where we teach children that killing another human being is wrong, but in certain circumstances it is right, such double standards lead to confusion. Of course, the content of this paragraph raises the argument with respect to relative and absolute values, and existing society attaches more importance to the former.

Having attempted to prove that sin is just as serious as a crime, it is opportune to examine the 'seven deadly sins.' The list of the seven sins is indexed in the following group of letters, **saligia:** *superbia* **(pride),** *avaritia* **(covetousness),** *Iuxuria* **(lust),** *invidia* **(envy),** *gula* **(gluttony),** *ira* **(anger),** *acedia* **(sloth).** **Gregory** called them the seven 'spirits of wickedness.' Pride is the worse sin of all, since it is the source of all the others. Pride leads to vainglory which is implicit in party political pride, national pride and racial pride.

Covetousness, envy and gluttony are fostered by the economic system. Lust is frequently dramatised on television. Sloth has been encouraged by the frequent use of the motor vehicle and television or the absence of control of television interferes with work, especially children's homework. Anger arises from frustration and interference which is assumed to be a personal attack; pride is the real cause.

Sin is a fact of human life and the wages of sin must be paid. Natural Law states, 'Never do to others what you would not like others to do to you.' Most human beings do not know what they do to others. Why not? Because you can only know others to the extent that you know yourself. Self-knowledge is the first great world in the four great worlds of knowledge:

(i)   the internal world of the first person;
(ii)   the internal world of other persons;
(iii)   the external world of the first person;
(iv)   the external world of other persons.

St Paul was aware of his internal world which is confirmed by his confession, 'My own behaviour perplexes me. For I know I wish to perform good acts but I find myself performing bad acts that I really loathe. I ponder; if I act in such a way when it is not my desire to act in that way, I do not understand, therefore it must be sin that has forced its way into my nature.' It remains true, human beings cannot eliminate sin, but they are given the means to reduce to the minimum their undesirable behaviour. In other words, human beings fall short of perfection which presents a difficult challenge for intentional goal-directed behaviour. It must be emphasised the efficiency of a human being depends upon his/her degree of persistence.

Reflecting upon **Dorothy Sayers** perception of society in 1957, here is a revised list of the *principia vitia* relating to existing society.

(1) *Government devoid of principles.* All power corrupts and power precedes principles.

(2) *Business devoid of ethics.* Maximum profit is the ultimate goal and all costs must be challenged, especially the labour cost.

(3) *Economics devoid of logic.* The logic of production and transport is not the logic of society.

(4) *Wealth devoid of distributive justice.* 'To them that hath much, more shall be given, and to them that hath little, more shall be taken away;' this is the maxim of existing society.

(5) *Science devoid of values.* Facts are more important than values is the conclusion of those in the field of science, yet where would science be without truth?

(6) *Religion devoid of a true creed.* 'Faith will move mountains,' but reason tells us that faith without action is futile. A true creed must be credible and consistent.

(7) *Knowledge devoid of self-knowledge.* Self-knowledge is dependent on the exclusion of all objects to become aware of the self. The steadfast pursuit of self-knowledge leads to the awakening of the **pure ego,** or the realisation of the divine asset within oneself. **Shakespeare** made Hamlet say:

> *This above all. To thine own self be true,*
> *And it must follow, as the night the day,*
> *Thou canst not be false to any man.*

Immanuel Kant maintained the moral law lies completely *apriori* in reason itself. When duty is the guide for human action, it requires more than an act as duty might have prescribed. There is a distinction between a person who acts from 'inclination' and one who acts from a 'sense of duty.' Suppose a young man promises to meet a young lady at a certain place and time, then he is under an obligation to keep that appointment. Suppose he regrets the arrangement he made and then has an 'inclination' to break the appointment without informing the young lady, then he has failed to fulfil the obligation. Promise-making produces an obligation whereas no speech or written act involves no obligation, so it reduces to 'inclination' as to the way a person acts. However, a 'sense of duty' relates to a man performing an act opposed by his 'inclination' or willingness, but consents to perform because he knows he ought to act without query. **Kant** conceived the moral law tied to duties and obligations of human beings.

He recognised that the consciousness of duty omits how a man ought to act in certain conditions and circumstances. He introduced the concepts of the *categorical imperative* and the *hypothetical imperative.* The 'hypothetical imperative' is defined thus: you must act in a certain way if you wish to achieve a certain end, The 'categorical imperative' eliminates the conditional if, therefore a certain type of action is unconditionally necessary with indifference to any end.

The 'categorical imperative' is both *apriori* and *synthetic.* The former meaning prior to experience; knowledge that is universal and necessary. The latter meaning that the predicate of the statement consists of information not contained in the subject. For example: 'trees are necessary for a forest' is not a *synthetic* statement; 'trees are necessary for human existence' is a *synthetic* statement. **Kant** expressed the 'categorical imperative' as follows: 'Act only in accordance with that maxim whereby thou can simultaneously will that your act should become a universal law.' Therefore, promise-keeping and truth-telling count as actions that obey the universal law, for in a world where broken promises and false statements were accepted as universal law, human relationships would degenerate into distrust, antagonism and violent reaction. In the political affairs of nations and in industrial affairs between the claims of capital and the claims of labour, there have been disastrous consequences when universal law is disobeyed.

Kant produced a supplement to the 'categorical imperative.' 'Act so as to treat humanity, whether in thine own person or in that of another, in every case as an end and never as a means.' Why treat a human being as an end? Because 'a good will is that by which alone human existence can have an absolute value; and in relation to it, the existence of the world can have an ultimate purpose.' Unfortunately, in many cases, human beings are treated as a means, as **Jean-Paul Sartre** observed; on many occasions, other persons treat us as physical objects instead of as human beings. In many cases, a human being is treated as a number when the unemployment statistics are promulgated; minimum regard is paid to the frustration, anguish or sometimes despair of a human being; consolation is offered by claiming that the rate of increase in unemployment is declining.

Arthur Schopenhauer believed that the 'Will' is the motive force in the universe but the cosmic will is evil. Therefore, more unhappiness than happiness must exist. There is a natural tendency for human beings to perpetuate their species although this leads to further suffering and death. This is the reason for the guilt that emerges from the one-flesh act. The intensity of the will, or the will to live is the struggle for existence which is the cause of all pain and suffering. To escape from this miserable condition, death is not the answer; **Schopenhauer**

believed that a condition of non-existence is necessary, or what the Buddhists call *Nirvana*.

In this mystical world, the meaning of love becomes transparent whereby sympathy and an acute awareness of the pain of other human beings dominates the mind. A good man is aware of the suffering of other human beings and he will act to help them rather than himself. The precondition to this good life is to reduce the power of the individual will until it is completely denied; then such a self-sacrifice is rewarded by harmony, peace and happiness. **Schopenhauer** thought that all individual wills are parts of the universal will, so that when human beings realise they struggle against themselves, then they might cease struggling and develop a new humanistic sensitivity.

Jeremy Bentham built his philosophy on two principles, the 'principle of association' and the 'principle of the greatest happiness.' The first principle related to his social system and in his association of ideas was the 'principle of utility' which he thought was an essential precondition to establishing a moral law. He followed the Epicureans by insisting that the good is equated with pleasure or happiness, and the bad is equated with pain. It must be pointed out that he made no distinction between pleasure and happiness. There is a flaw in **Bentham's** social system. If every man pursues his own pleasure or happiness, how are we to consider the happiness of mankind. Further, if every man pursues his own happiness, and in the course, may harm others, such as noise pollution from pop music transmitted by high powered amplifiers, the Utilitarian doctrine cancels Kantian doctrine which says, 'You ought not to do this.'

In his book *Utilitarianism*, **John Stuart Mill** wrote, 'If I am asked what I mean by difference of quality in pleasure, or what makes a pleasure more valuable than another, merely as a pleasure, except its being greater in amount, there is no possible answer. Of two pleasures, if there be one to which all or almost all who have experience of both give a decided preference, irrespective of any feeling of moral obligation to prefer it, that is the more desirable pleasure.' His argument that virtue depends on utility is fallacious. Drugs are a means to cure certain health problems, so they are certainly useful. However, in the world today, a great number of human beings pursue the pleasure obtained from drugs and the desire for the pleasure obtained leads them into crime to pay for the drugs. The 'principle of utility' can never be equated with virtue. This restrictive doctrine is known as *hedonistic utilitarianism.* The formula of **Bentham** says that we should pursue the greatest good or the greatest happiness of the greatest number. This formula is flawed since if we attempt to spread happiness to a great number of persons, we may produce less happiness than if we concentrated on a smaller number of persons. If we have ten loaves to be distributed amongst ten thousand starving children, what happiness would we produce by giving each child a few crumbs?

One philosopher, **George Moore,** perceived the weakness in the 'theory of utilitarianism' and insisted that preventing misery is far more important than producing happiness. In his *Principia Ethica,* he claimed that it was impossible to analyse the 'good,' therefore it was indefinable; a 'Naturalistic Fallacy' emerges when an attempt is made to define any moral words. **Dr AC Ewing** asserted that the 'theory of utilitarianism' may be condemned as not reconcilable with the dictates of 'Justice.' The principle informs us to produce as much happiness as possible for the greatest number, thus implying that the way happiness is distributed does not matter (some will be left out). However, 'Justice' requires that of the two distributions, we ought to prefer the fair to the unfair. The 'utilitarian principle' ignores the fair distribution of happiness. Utilitarianism has been identified as a political philosophy, and it is associated with democratic government.

Nietzsche observed that in the 'utilitarian doctrine,' some human beings are valued more highly than others. Another serious criticism of 'utilitarianism' is that it disregards the motives of human action. Can an act be right when an individual is cheated or exploited by a number of persons who benefit by the evil action? Utilitarianism is a relative doctrine in which moral behaviour is associated solely with the desirable effect of an act irrespective of the motive of the act.

Again, referring to *Principia Ethica,* Professor GE Moore presented an argument opposing *egoistic hedonism.* One's own pleasure is the only good existing, maintains the egoistical hedonist. If this is true, what applies to the egoistical hedonist applies to every other person in the world today; so, we are drawn to the preposterous conclusion that every one of five billion things is the one and only thing good-in-itself.

Unselfishness or consideration of another person's happiness relates to the ethics of Jesus Christ. It involves personal sacrifice, but like *egoistic hedonism,* there is a limit. As Dr AC Ewing pointed out, 'A society in which everybody spent his/her life sacrificing all his/her pleasure for others would be even more absurd than a society whose members all lived by taking in each other's washing.

This suggests the view that self-sacrifice is only required or indeed justified where it is necessary in order to secure for somebody else a *greater* good than that sacrificed. We cannot define an unselfish man as one who sacrifices his welfare to others, but only as one who does so within reason.' Certainly, the conception of the unselfish man implicates human limitations; limitation of knowledge, limitation of energy and the limitation of benevolence. If any human being was entirely unselfish, then he or she would die from starvation; the point is, such extreme philanthropy is short-lived.

Naturalism attempts to free ethics from its 'uncertainty' predicament by suggesting that ethical terms can be analysed into non-ethical terms: also, ethical conclusions can be deduced from non-ethical premises. *Naturalism* identifies three forms of hedonism.

(i)   The pleasure of the agent. (Egoistic Hedonism)
(ii) The pleasure of the receiver. (Altruistic Hedonism)
(iii) The pleasure of the greatest number. (Utilitarianism)

The approach and attitude to moral problems by the means of the doctrine of *naturalism* is similar to *descriptivism* which entails the belief that ethical statements have meaning in the same way as factual statements. An alternative doctrine to *naturalism* is *relativism.* However, *relativism* does not allow reasonable discussion for it is dogmatised that all values are relative. **Ortegay Gasset** wrote in *The Modern Theme,* 'If truth does not exist, *relativism* cannot take itself seriously; belief in truth is a deeply-rooted foundation of human life; if we remove it, life is converted into an illusion and an absurdity.'

RM Hare, in arguing for 'Objective Prescriptions' wrote, 'The idea that only some kind of *descriptivism*—some kind of factuality in moral judgements—can make objectivity possible rests on a very fundamental mistake which nearly everybody commits who studies the question. I think…today moral philosophers fall for the most part into two camps. One lot says that, because moral judgements do not state facts, any kind of moral reasoning is impossible…The other lot says that since moral reasoning is possible, moral judgements must state facts.' He continued later, 'The most common mistake of would-be objectivists is to treat the word 'objective' as if it meant the same as factual.'

Subjectivism is the view that what are claimed as objective truths or laws are merely concealed commands or expressions of emotion. Objectivism is the opinion that truths exist independent of desires, beliefs and wishes, so that any distinction between moral and factual statements is denied.

James Griffin argued that it is impossible to obtain substantive moral principles from the logic of the basic moral concepts without the aid of 'some substantive beliefs.' Further, he maintained that to choose a different definition of ethics to accommodate the management of facts is impossible without 'some substantive beliefs guiding the choice.' **James Griffin** insisted, 'We have no method for ethics, unless we can identify beliefs of special reliability.'

The logic of absolutism includes the assertion that some kinds of actions are always wrong, and that the 'law of excluded middle' must take into account ethical propositions. Can any rational human being deny this proposition is true? **'War is evil.'** For absolutists, truth is essential in ethics and the Greek poet, **Sophocles** words appertaining to the moral laws are paraphrased below:

> *They were born not in man's mind,*
> *Mortal parents you will not find,*
> *Nor shall man's forgetfulness ever make them sleep,*
> *God's laws were made for all to keep.*

Chapter 6
State and Society

The title of this chapter could well be changed to 'Politics and People,' as it is analogous to the chosen title. However, it is the writer's intention to start with the origin of society, so the existing title is justified.

No human being can bear to be isolated from other human beings for a long period. Primitive men and women living in caves or otherwise, preferred to be close to their own species. The instinctive belief prevailing at that time is related to this proposition; there is more safety in numbers. Defence against wild animals and hostile tribes forced a fearful person to join a group to organise themselves against attacks and to co-operate in the procurement of food and water.

Inevitably, disagreements occurred appertaining to the desire and purpose of certain activities, so a scant form of society was established. Now, it is unfeasible to live in a group without social discipline, thus by a crude method of communication, a few patterns of social behaviour were developed. The first requirement in any form of society is to introduce simple rules that are approved by its members. From this root, the branches of tribal laws and customs began to grow. This unwritten system of society demanded obedience and any member who failed to obey was severely punished, most frequently without mercy as capital punishment was employed as a means of deterrence.

As the society grew larger, the time arrived for the laws and customs to be written down. Of course, this was not possible until the evolution of language and problem-solving intelligence had reached a certain level. As the early economies developed, it was perceived that the area of territory is an economic necessity, thus the area required to produce food and resources for a social group became highly significant. Fights over territory increased in frequency as deficiencies in resources became apparent. Language assisted human beings to advance the ideas on property and rightful ownership which became a special part of law.

A deliberate error of omission has been made concerning two questions that are inextricably linked to the constitution of the State and what powers should be entrusted to the State. During the period of development of social organisation, disputes kept arising about the nature of the laws and who should devise them. Philosophers have asked how the State came into existence and is there a divine origin?

In the early days of the construction of a State, it was accepted by its citizens that those who gained power to dictate to them had been given laws by the Gods. The illustrious example is recorded when Moses ascended Mount Sinai to receive the ten laws from the Hebrew God, Jehovah. The Ten Commandments formed the framework of Hebrew law and the impressive point is the belief that they were God-made and not man-made. There was a certain advantage in this arrangement, for anyone breaking the law would not only be punished by man but also by a God of Wrath. This situation existed in other States where citizens believed in the divine origination of the State complete with divine laws, which if disobeyed, then divine punishment was exercised.

Greek history revealed another question that has attracted attention of political philosophers—is the citizen more important than the State or is the State more important than the citizen? The ancient Greeks believed in the latter as experience showed that a citizen's life was of short duration and belonging to a group was more beneficial than otherwise. The preservation of the group overruled the claim of the individual. Incitement to rebel or protest was not tolerated, for slave labour was devoid of human rights.

The Pythagorean doctrine was consistent with the situation described as it possessed an aristocratic nature, for the Pythagoreans despised the masses and proclaimed anarchy as the greatest evil. **Democritus,** the leader of the Atomists agreed with the Pythagoreans emphasising that a well-ordered State was a great asset. He is said to be the author of many wise statements, 'When the State is in a healthy condition, all things prosper; when it is corrupt, all things go to ruin.' Such a statement is inconsistent with his materialistic philosophy for he conceived thought as a physical process and the universe without purpose. Therefore, a fundamental political question arises—what is the ultimate purpose for the existence of any form of government?

It has been argued that patriotism involves blind loyalty to the State and it is synonymous with the opinion 'my country is always right'. Sooner or later, some men of free spirit began to query this divine right of the State to dominate citizens and claimed that the citizen had a right to criticise the State. The Sophists were the first to support the individual which was confirmed by **Protagoras**, 'Man is the measure of all things.' In the dialogue '**Gorgias**,' a distinguished orator at that time is reputed to have said that all great men of history had one thing in common, all broke the laws of their totalitarian state that had set in place pillars of oppression. Unfortunately, such actions were treated as rebellions against the State, so the Sophists, although highlighting the problem were unable to offer a solution because they maintained that all knowledge is subjective.

Socrates teaching method involved constantly asking many questions: What is a State? What is the purpose of the State? Who should rule? Although he gave no answer to these questions, he perceived his method as a means for citizens to seek true knowledge. What is true knowledge? For **Socrates**, there was a close relation between knowledge and virtue as knowledge without virtue is mere vanity.

Socrates was accused of corrupting the youth of Athens whereupon the Tribunal found him guilty, but prior to his sentence of death, he informed the judges that if they would not permit him to associate with the young men of Athens, then:

I should reply: *Men of Athens, I honour and love you; but I shall obey God rather than you, and while I have life and strength, I shall not cease from the practice and teaching of philosophy, exhorting anyone whom I meet and by saying to him as my habit is: You, my dear friend—a citizen of the great and mighty and wise city of Athens—are you not ashamed of trying to get as much money, honour and reputation as possible, while remaining careless and indifferent to wisdom and truth and the greatest perfection of your soul? For I know this is the commandment of God; and I believe that no greater good has ever happened to Athens than my service to God.*

Socrates developed an exceptional character and it is doubtful if any other past philosopher has lived his own philosophy like Socrates. He became resigned to his death and he continued one of the greatest speeches ever made by a human being which is a significant milestone in western culture.

There is great reason to hope that death is good; for either death is a state of nothingness and utter unconsciousness, or, as men say, there is a change and migration of the soul from this world to another...I see clearly the time has arrived when it is better for me to die and be released from trouble. And so, I am not angry with those who condemned and those who accused me; they have done me no harm, although they did not mean to do me any good; and for this I may gently blame them. But I have a favour to ask them. When my sons are grown up, punish them and trouble them, as I have troubled you, if they seem to care about riches, or anything, more than about virtue; or if they pretend to be something when they are really nothing—then reprove them as I have reproved you, for not caring about that for which you ought to care, and thinking that they are something when they are really nothing. And if you do this, both my sons and I will have received justice at your hands. The hour of departure has arrived, and we go our separate ways—I to die, and you to live. Which is better, only God knows.

At the end of the 'Phaedo,' these words were uttered in tribute to **Socrates** who was a man that practiced what he preached: 'Of all the men of his time whom I have known, he was the wisest, the most just and the best.' This tragic event had a profound effect upon **Plato** who recognised that 'politics is full of dishonesty and hypocrisy and is no place for an honest man.'

Plato's impressive dialogue, the 'Republic,' contains his theory of the state. He believed that virtue ought to guide the actions of men, and he thought that virtue in the state is equated to justice. This awakens men to the concept of humanity, and in his dialogue, he refers to justice as the health of the individual soul; he defines ethics as an inquiry into justice.

One of the greatest authorities on Plato was **FM Cornford.** In 'The Unwritten Philosophy,' he clearly explained the choice confronting man in the building of an ideal society: 'There are two ways in which a man may approach the task of conceiving an ideal society. One is to start with the reformation of the individual, and then to imagine a society containing perfect individuals. That is the logical outcome of **Socrates's** mission to his fellow citizens described in the *Apology.* The other is to take human nature as we find it, and to construct a social order that will make the best of it as it is and as seems likely to remain. This is the course taken by **Plato** in the *Republic.'*

Plato divided men into three divisions. First, there are those solely occupied in acquiring money, and of course, the pleasures that money can buy. Second, there are those who are primarily interested in gaining power and honour derived from such power. Third, there are those who find no satisfaction in the pursuit of money or power, but prefer to spend their time in the contemplation of truth, beauty and goodness; in other words, the pursuit of values.

Inevitably, **Plato** was in favour of an aristocratic approach as the only possible option for any theory and constitution of the state. The deep perception of **Plato** convinced him that Athens was perishing due to the egotism of men with vested interests, so he came to the conclusion that the evil must be severed at the root. In the *Republic,* **Socrates** is given the role to make this famous statement, 'Unless either the lovers of wisdom become rulers in their cities, or those who are now rulers come to love wisdom in the true sense and in sufficient measure—unless in fact, political power and the pursuit of wisdom be united in the same persons, while the many natures of those who pursue the one to the exclusion of the other are forcibly prohibited from pursuing either separately, there can be no rest from troubles for the race of mankind.'

Plato, in arguing that the qualification for the government posts must be related to the superior minds and the better souls, he realised that philosophers are human beings, and not perfect, therefore they can make errors of judgement. The chief error is that a philosopher may be tempted by pride to capture power. **Plato**, when present at the trial of **Socrates** witnessed the foul use of power and he expressed his thoughts about the temptation to gain power: 'no human soul…will be able to resist the temptation of arbitrary power—there is no one who will not, under such circumstances, become filled with folly, the worst of diseases, and be hated by his nearest and dearest friends; and when this happens, his kingdom is undermined so that all his power vanishes.'

For some cryptic reason, the two main concepts of democracy have not received equal attention. Liberty has overshadowed equality, due to the fact that the concept of equality is subject to significant differences. Two skilled men with identical physical characteristics are given the task to make a mortise and tenon joint by hand; one will make a far better job than the other, therefore indicating an inequality in skill. Two pianists may play the same musical composition, striking the same notes, but one performance may sound like a mathematical progression of notes, whereas the other performance may produce an aesthetic feeling of the divine. Equality in the context of distributive justice and undeserved inequality ought to be highlighted more by academics. There is a delicate balance between liberty and equality, so intervention is necessary to balance the scales. The intervention factor is *fraternity* which is related to the spiritual world and not the material world. Alas! 'All men are brothers' has been replaced by 'All men are competitors.'

Both **Confucius** and **Plato** refer to a great idea which has a reality beyond most human conception. **Plato** expressed it in the idea of the 'supreme good,' and **Confucius** identified it as the 'Tao' (the way). Their political systems were both authoritarian and anti-democratic. **Plato** would have agreed with the conclusion drawn by **Confucius**—'Remove the rules of propriety and justice, then watch how men treat each other.'

In the first book of his *Politics,* **Aristotle** refers to the task of finding the best form of the State, namely, the one in which man can be most virtuous. He returned to the simple analogy of the state with the union of man and woman who cannot live without each other, that is the household. Out of the union of several households emerges a village and out of the union of many villages emerges a State. This led **Aristotle** to assert that nature compels man to be a social creature, and the greatest benefactor to society was he who laid the foundation of the State, for without justice, man is the worst of creatures. **Aristotle** wrote, 'The end of the State is the good life' which conveyed a far different meaning to the good life pursued today.

Aristotle accepted that all transactions were conducted with money but wealth was not the collection of coin. 'The most hated sort, and with the greatest reason, is usury, which makes gain out of money itself, and not from the natural object of it. Money was intended to be used in exchange, but not to increase at interest *beyond a reasonable percentage rate.* This is the controversial question which has defied a precise answer—what is a reasonable percentage rate avoiding usury?'

The advent of the Christians changed the attitude towards the State, for a Christian's first loyalty was to God and the laws of God. For many, the affairs of the State gave them little comfort, so they escaped from their unhealthy environment to a holy environment where they were able to nurture their souls in the monastic way of life. Of course, such a way of life afforded ample time for some to concentrate on theological doctrine while others were teaching the Christian doctrine.

As the Christian doctrine spread throughout the Roman Empire, the monastic attitude of world-denial could not be maintained for the development of the church as an institution required the management of property and wealth. This change from forsaking the temporal world caused problems for the Catholic Church. **Bishop Ambrose** was convinced that the ownership of property and wealth was 'damnable.' His younger friend, **Augustine**, agreed that the acquisition of wealth could interfere with the Christian way of life, but he thought that everyone had the right to acquire wealth. He specified no limit.

In his 'City of God,' **Augustine** made it clear that the State is inferior to the church, so a theocracy was established. In this holy system, the Pope became the divine guide of the Catholic Church, charged with the power to dominate all the sovereigns of the States. Although a sovereign may commit errors of judgement, the Pope cannot commit such errors. **Augustine** placed a huge burden of responsibility on the Pope claiming that he was infallible because he was the agent for God in the world.

During the course of the Dark Ages, any tendency towards individualism was suppressed and the divine king sat upon the throne and his authority could not be challenged. After the first millennium of Christianity, two groups of scholars emerged who differed about determining the status of universals. Objects in the world have common characteristics and it is in the nature of nearly all characteristics to actually characterise a multitude of objects. Realism is related to *universalia ante res;* universals prior to the object(s); Nominalism is related to *universalia post res;* universals after, or obtained from the object(s). **Anselm,** a leading realist maintained that universals experience a reality limited to themselves. However, **Roscellinus** contended that universals are abstractions of things or merely empty names. The Nominalists were accused of heresy and it was pointed out that whoever ascribes more reality to things than to ideas is more attached to this world than to the ideal kingdom of heaven. These two viewpoints were associated with the problem of the State and the citizens. All the parts make the whole, but the Realists claimed that the whole is the only reality whereas the Nominalists claimed that the parts are the only reality, and the whole is just a name. By substitution, the Realists accepted that the State was the only reality whereas the Nominalists accepted that the citizens were the only reality. Division of opinion alternated between the notion that real power resides in the State, and the notion that real power resides in the citizen because, after all, the State is made up of a multitude of citizens.

Yet again, out of the thesis and antithesis confrontation, came the synthesis. **Pierre Abelard** in his famous book *Sic et Non*, produced a dialectical argument in which he claimed that logic takes its name from the *logos,* that is from Jesus Christ. In bringing the strife between the Realists and Nominalists to an end, he referred to the fact that we speak of identity and difference in respect to resemblance. Things resemble each other, so from this resemblance, a universal is derived. However, it must be emphasised that the resemblance between two like things cannot be considered itself a thing. **Plato** claimed that the universal is subject to two conditions—either it is external to its object, or it is internal to its object and therefore fragmented. **Abelard** produced his own formula, *universalia sunt in rebus;* universals are ideas within and compiled by the mind. This doctrine is known as *conceptualism* because someone called the universals *conceptus.*

Applying the doctrine to the State, it was realised that the citizens could no longer be disregarded, but neither could the State be disregarded, as an individual citizen was a part of the State. Further, a State educational system was a social and spiritual enterprise in which an individual citizen could teach others or receive instructions from others. **Abelard** was labelled a *Nominalist* but he refuted this and also said that without doubt, **Rosellinus's** view, that only the individual exists, is absurd. Nevertheless, the seed had been sown and more citizens began to criticise the authority of the State and the church.

Thomas Aquinas declared that God is the end of all things, so that the church has a greater role than the State in God's government. He claimed that by nature, man is a political being, therefore, desires to be a part of society. All action has the good as its end, so that evil as such cannot be willed, He believed in a centralised government with a monarch as a head, but a citizen's ultimate loyalty was to the church and God. The government of the world is related differently to rational and irrational creatures. To the former are given laws, the latter are compelled by laws; the former are treated as ends, the latter as means. Love to God and to one's neighbour forms the essential content of the law. Since this is the end of man, the natural and the divine laws coincide and it is false to base what is right only upon divine ordinance and not upon nature. Punishment threatened by God in part as satisfaction, in part as a warning, may be exercised by the authorities as servants of God. It is astonishing to learn that **Aquinas** was critical of those who supported the abolition of capital punishment. **Niccolo Machiavelli,** nicknamed Old Nick, desired to see established an Italian nation completely independent of the church. He maintained that of all peoples, the Latin were the most corrupt, hence, the only hope left was for one man to possess absolute power. Now power is nearly always linked to public opinion which is manipulated by propaganda, implying that the authors of the propaganda are free from sin and corruption. **Machiavelli** identified this process of manipulation used by the Catholic Church to increase its power in the centuries prior to the Reformation.

To preserve the monarchy, national conscription must be introduced. The ruler must guard against those crimes which embitter the minds of the people inciting attacks upon private property. The ruler guards against these attacks if he never forgets that all men are wicked, and most of them are stupid, and if he acts accordingly, he will preserve his power. Machiavelli, besides affirming that a ruler possessed the right to use any means to achieve his ends, insisted that a ruler must imitate the fox in deceit and the lion in cruelty. Paradoxically, we live in an irrational society yet some of its members are rational. The constitution of the state may be that of a democracy or a dictatorship.

Hugo Grotius declared; to understand natural right or law, it is the law which is not arbitrarily established by God or men, but which follows necessarily from the nature of man. By his proper nature though, that nature which distinguishes him from the beasts, man who for that reason has the faculty of speech and language, is destined for society, that is, for quiet, rationally ordered society. Therefore, everything which is at strife with such an ordered society of rational beings is unlawful. To live in such a society, a man must sacrifice certain natural rights, such as the right to unlimited freedom of action.

Thomas Hobbes or affectionately nicknamed Old Tom in some circles, is commonly known as a naturalistic political philosopher. He displayed antagonism towards scholasticism by asserting that since theology had sprung from supernatural revelation and not from reason, it was at once excluded from philosophy. The intermingling of the two, of faith and reason, is a sin against both.

In the 'Leviathan,' **Thomas Hobbes** dogmatised that since self-preservation is the first law of nature for individuals, so likewise, it is nature's first law for a sum of individuals to seek security, but this conflicts with the fundamental law of nature. This fundamental law affirms that man has complete freedom of action, or the natural right to do anything that satisfies his desire; restraint is not an option.

As security is incompatible with the natural freedom for all to do anything which pleases them, it only remains that each person should renounce their freedom on the condition that others do likewise. This proposed contract, was not what had been said by **Aristotle** and **Grotius**, a consequence of the social tendency or the love of one's countrymen, but due to the fear and care for self-interest. With respect to the laws of society, without democracy, tyranny will raise its ugly head and when tyranny arises the only remedy is the act of rebellion. The laws have to be enforced and absolute power is required for the enforcement of laws.

The contract or covenant includes the agreement for the imposition of an absolute monarchy. However, the covenant is not made between the citizens and the sovereign, it is made between the citizens themselves, and they must choose whether to transfer power to a single ruler or live in a chaotic society. When the citizens have exercised this specific freedom of choice, they forfeit any right to political power. When the act of subjection is set up by nature, so founded upon force, we have patriarchal government. On the other hand, when it is self-determined and contracted, we have a state. The monarch is not tied to the contract because his contract is with God, hence religious freedom is prohibited. The religion of the citizens is dependent upon the religion of the monarch. This loyal support for the English monarchy elicited the controversial supposition of the 'divine right of kings' connected to the tenet, 'the king is incapable of doing wrong.' Such a man would be more than a king, he would be a saint.

John Locke completes this trio of distinct political philosophers. Old John rejected Old Tom's assertion that the natural state of man was one where selfish egoism inevitably leads to conflict. He contended that man is not completely selfish as on occasions, he considers the welfare of others as well as co-operating with others, although frequently man is prone to selfish egoism. In his 'Treatise on Civil Government,' **Locke** wrote, 'Men living together according to reason, without a common superior on earth, with authority to judge between them, is properly the state of nature…The state of nature has a law of nature to govern it, which obliges every one; and reason, which is that law, teaches all mankind, who will but consult it, that being all equal and independent, no one ought to harm another in his life, health, liberty, or possessions.'

Locke acknowledged that a state of war may arise from a state of nature, dependent upon conditions and circumstances. The case where the monarch desires absolute power over his subjects or the denial of all political freedom, such a case shows that a condition exists for a state of war. He assumed, 'The beginning of politic society depends upon the consent of the individuals to join into and make one society…Political power I take to be the right of making laws, with penalty of death, and consequently all less penalties for the regulating and preserving of property, and employing the force of the community in the execution of such laws, and in defence of the commonwealth from foreign injury, and all this only for the public good.'

Laws which have been devised by the representatives of the citizens and made known to all of them are called 'democratic government.' The legislature should be prevented from executing the laws, so the legislature and executive should be made independent bodies for the public good. Undoubtedly, **Locke's** political philosophy was a power of influence. From a critical analysis of his 'Treatise,' serious shortcomings are recognised. First, he was silent about the function of the judiciary; second, he referred to the 'public good' without mentioning what contributes to it; next, he appeared to have a strong attachment to property and he failed to foresee that individuals would become subservient to large corporations; the farming lobby, the transport lobby and the nuclear industry lobby have far greater power of persuasion than any individual. **Locke's** change from government by decree to government by consent where the state's power was diminished produced the clarion call—the less state interference the better. In his 'Wealth of Nations,' **Adam Smith** argued that there is no better state than when men are occupied in the affairs of unrestricted competition, freedom of exchange and enlightened self-interest. His *laissez faire* doctrine claimed that an individual possesses a natural right to pursue economic goals with the minimum of state intervention.

Since **Plato**, this argument about the power of the State versus the power of the individual may be compared to a 'tug of war.' Freedom became the cry of the masses, but they never indicated 'freedom from what?' or 'freedom to do what?' **Voltaire** had an abundance of enthusiasm for human freedom, yet he rejected the idea that the proletariat were fit for self-government. He thought that the 'ignorant rabble' were inclined to be philistines and also a danger when the bridle of restraint was removed.

Rousseau opposed **Voltaire's** viewpoint as he believed in the complete freedom of the individual. In his book called the *Social Contract*, the first chapter contains these words, 'Man is born free, and everywhere he is in chains. One man thinks he is the master of others, but remains more of a slave than they are.'

He preferred direct government to representative government, and thought that democracy is nothing more than an 'elective aristocracy.' Most philosophers have a dream of reforming society, but before this can be achieved, the individual must be reformed.

John Stuart Mill gave much attention to the problem of reforming society and the following paragraph is extracted from his 'Autobiography': *While we repudiated with the greatest energy that tyranny of society over the individual which most Socialistic systems are supposed to involve, we yet look forward to a time when society will no longer be divided into the idle and the industrious; when the rule that they who do not work shall not eat will be applied not to paupers only, but impartially to all; when the division of the produce of labour, instead of depending, as in so great a degree it now does, on the accident of birth, will be made concert on an acknowledged principle of justice. The social problem of the future, we considered to be: how to unite the greatest individual liberty of action, with a common ownership in the raw materials of the globe, and the equal participation of all in the benefits of combined labour.* **Mill** perceived that the raw materials of the Earth should not be in the balance sheet of a few international corporations. A further problem that he recognised which exists throughout the world today is the distinction between unentitled poverty and unentitled wealth. Surely, a just society is concerned with the distribution of wealth amongst all its members.

In his famous essay 'On Liberty,' **Mill** focused attention on a serious defect in the democratic system. In such a system, the majority always rules. Now, when the majority power is not restrained then tyranny in different clothes emerges; that is, the tyranny of the majority over minority parties. This tyranny tends to arise, either from pressure upon the government to introduce laws to quell quarrelsome groups or from the exertion of public opinion, even though they cannot be justified morally or rationally. For **Mill**, it became evident that when the majority were given too much power to dominate, then toleration was tested to the limit. A harm criterion was formulated by him: 'The sole end for which mankind are warranted individually or collectively, in the interference of the actions of any of their number, is self-protection. That is the only purpose for which power can be rightfully exercised over any member of a civilised community, against his will, is to prevent harm to others. His own good, either physical or moral is not a sufficient warrant.'

Mill foresaw the development in mass communication and the increase in the circulation of newspapers, all engaged in the manipulation of public opinion. He wrote, 'The masses have their thinking done for them, by men much like themselves, addressing them or speaking in their name, on the spur of the moment, through the newspapers.' It has been observed that intellectual trickery is an instrument used by politicians. All governments as well as opposition parties control a propaganda machine. The classic example of the efficiency of these propaganda machines was the way the government and opposition parties squashed the question, 'Ought man to split atoms?' Future historians will record that this was the era when man took over the role of God.

Both **Hegel** and **Marx** pointed to a serious problem in society. **Hegel** pointed to our alienation from God, our alienation from our neighbour, and **Marx** pointed to the alienation from work acquaintances in the industrial system. Certainly, society's acceptance of materialism and individualism has added to the problem which is spiritual in nature. Typically, man has followed the political pendulum from right to left, from one extreme to the other. As the ecological consequences of our production/consumption system conflict more and more with nature, then it may be realised that a balance must be struck between the state and the individual.

Nothing can be fully understood without reference to context; in other words, to understand the present problems of existing British society, we must know something about the past out of which the problems have developed. Ask any student of history what significant event occurred in 1776 and the reply will most surely be—'The American Declaration of Independence' was signed. However, in Britain, an event occurred which was the origin of the industrial revolution. **James Watt** invented the steam engine. Although it paved the way for a railway system, it signalled the beginning of momentous change. A new class emerged called the 'masters' who possessed the capital to buy all the new machines; Hargreaves' spinning jenny, Arkwright's water frame and Crompton's spinning mule. Crompton worked for five years to perfect his invention which produced the finest muslin yarn, yet while others became wealthy by using similar machines, he ended his days in virtual poverty.

The Capitalists all had the same policy-maximisation of income from the minimisation of cost. Adult males expected a man's wage which had to be eliminated in the efficiency drive of the masters, so they employed children. Employment is the wrong word, they exploited children who either worked like slaves or starved. After a long period of protest and agitation by the church leaders and humanitarians, a child-labour bill was passed in 1819. It prohibited the employment of children under the age of nine.

It is necessary to refer to this past incredible action to verify that capitalism has always required a cheap source of labour. Capitalism and labour can never exist in harmony until justice becomes the reality instead of a mere word.

A new religion emerged—the religion of 'Manchesterism.' The doctrine insisted that capitalism was the ideal economic system because it conformed to the 'Laws of Nature.' It was argued thus: the generator of capitalism was 'enlightened self-interest' which relates to me—first and most, or in plain language, mere 'greed.' The maintenance of the system was achieved via competition. The capitalists argued, 'Can it be denied that greed is instinctive in human nature?' Further, can it be denied that competition is instinctive in animal nature? Prices were dictated by the absolute law of 'supply and demand.' Wages had to be kept low to allow the 'masters' to compete effectively and preserve their profits. The health and safety of employees was ignored. The French phrase was imported, *laissez faire;* the translation was parallel to 'free for all,' but the reality was 'free for a few.' In the 1820s, the power of decision-making belonged to the Tories, who were mainly land-owners. The enterprising capitalists pressed for 'liberalism' in government which primarily reduced to liberation from government interference. The Tories were responsible for the high price of bread at that time, for they had introduced an outrageous tariff on wheat in order to protect their farming interests. The *Whigs* appealed to the masses about the gross unfairness and they easily won the support of the masses. 'Give us our daily bread at a reasonable price,' came the cry from the citizens. The 'Corn Laws' were repealed and after two rejections, the first 'Reform Bill' was passed in 1832; town dwellers who paid a rent of £10 or more were given the right to vote. For those who have little knowledge of political history, an important point to emphasise is that the limited franchise applied to adult males only who were able to pay a substantial rent. This reform amounted to a harsh, limited form of democracy and sex discrimination.

The Chartist Movement was founded by **William Lovett** and **Feargus O'Connor** who via the 'People's Charter' pressed for mankind suffrage, vote by ballot, and the payment of Members of Parliament. A refusal by the government to accept a petition caused frustration and agitation throughout the land. The protest of the working class was directed against the repression in political affairs and the oppression in social affairs. The second 'Reform Bill' of 1867 reduced the rent qualification from £10 to £5 per year and extended the franchise to lodgers who paid an annual rent of £10. The third 'Reform Bill' or the 'Franchise Act' of 1884 extended the franchise to all householders as well as rural labourers. Unfortunately, women were not considered as joint householders.

In 1918, the 'Representation of the People Act' allowed all adult male householders and all women over the age of thirty, the right to vote. Such outrageous discrimination led to the Suffragette Movement, so eventually in 1928, another Act gave women the same voting rights as men. The industrial revolution had progressed for 150 years since James Watt invented the steam engine, but the General Strike in 1926 showed that democracy had not improved the lot of the working class. **Thorstein Veblen** observed the consequences where businessmen dictate and the pursuit of profit is the primary goal in society. He wrote: 'The machine and their master, is no respecter of persons and knows neither morality nor dignity nor prescriptive right, divine or human.'

In his 'Theory of Justice,' **John Rawls** made two principles:

(i) Each person is to have an equal right to the most extensive basic liberty compatible with a similar liberty for others.
(ii) Social and economic inequalities are to be arranged so that:
    (a) they are to the greatest benefit of the least advantage and
    (b) they are attached to offices and positions with equality of opportunity for all.

Liberty must be protected before the second principle can come into operation. **Rawls** made a noble attempt to produce a valid 'theory of justice,' but where he floundered was in his basic 'principle of priority,' when a contest arises between liberty and equality, then liberty must always win. The polar concepts, liberty and equality have equal importance in a true democracy; therefore, any 'theory of justice' must seek an equilibrium. In his book, *Anarchy, State and Utopia*, **Robert Nozick** reveals an attitude similar to the early Whigs. He not only opposes any argument for equality but he is against any principle of distributive justice involving the distribution of goods in society. He claimed that individuals possess rights and they are inalienable rights; the right not to be injured; the right not to have their liberty limited; the right not to have their property taken without their consent. He insisted that these rights are jeopardised if the desire for equality is to be satisfied. The State must act as a 'night watchman' and it should not be engaged in social welfare.

Ronald Dworkin wrote his book with the express purpose of arguing that our basic liberties which are natural rights are not in conflict **with** equality. **Dworkin** appealed to liberals to reject **Bentham** as the true father of liberation for **Kant's** conception of human nature was in close proximity to **Plato's** conception. Liberty and equality may be compared to the two concepts in education, freedom and obedience. In existing society, our schools are in crisis; there is widespread truancy or alternatively, shirking duty; there is a lack of discipline or a refusal to obey the rules; and there is classroom violence or total irresponsibility by some pupils. Here is a classic case where too much freedom leads to a madhouse. However, too little freedom leads to a reformatory. These are the current twin problems; in politics, equality has been more or less disregarded; in education, discipline has been neglected; in both cases, there has been an excess of liberty. Liberty and equality; freedom and discipline; there is a delicate balance between the two sets of polar concepts. They are different to the polar concepts, good and bad, right and wrong. Here, no balancing act is required, one concept dominates the other. We value the good as opposed to the bad; we value right actions as opposed to wrong actions; we value our liberty but not the consequences of too much liberty.

It is a short step now to the consideration of rights, natural and human. What is the difference? As it is our nature to be allied to our species, then human rights are equivalent to natural rights according to **John Locke.** He thought there were three natural rights—the right to life, the right to liberty, and the right to property. The idea that in a state of nature, human beings can claim rights is wishful thinking. Without some power to protect rights, they are just futile.

Jeremy Bentham referred to the nonsense, 'How stands the truth of things? That there are such things as natural rights—no such things as rights anterior to the establishment of government—no such things as natural rights opposed to, in contradistinction to legal; that the expression is merely figurative—and living without government is to live without rights.' What governs the choice of rights? Inevitably, natural rights will be superseded by moral rights. However, **Locke's** first natural right, the right to life, means that we value human life. If this is so, then it must be a life with a distinctive human quality. Moreover, the right to life must implicate the right to appropriate environment devoid of air and water pollution. Of course, when we introduce air and water into the argument, we recognise that they are basic human needs. So, here we discover a connection between rights and needs. Conventional rights are entirely different to natural rights, they depend upon man-made law or other social institutions.

Alan Gewirth made a meritorious attempt to illustrate how human beings have rights to freedom and well-being. Natural rights **are** equivalent to foundational rights which are derived from **natural law.** Gewirth argued that freedom is good, likewise, human well-being is good. Now surely, the 'good' is central in *axiological ethics* or an ethics based primarily on value. The Platonic values are the highest system of ends, which involve the pursuit of the 'good.' Too much freedom or too little freedom can be equally as bad as **Plato** came to realise. Therefore, to claim I must have freedom without indicating 'freedom to do what' is unacceptable. Even the right to 'free speech' is contestable when the right involves the use of foul and abusive language that may cause psychological harm to a person. As **Alan Gewirth** should know, freedom is a matter of degree as no person can have unlimited freedom.

In the third statement, the jump across the fact/value gap is a leap from a need to a right, or a need for freedom, for without limited freedom we are in chains. Freedom is defined as the absence of restraint but laws are established to restrain.

When **Plato** referred to the 'Justice in the human soul,' he meant it relates to the spiritual part of man involving his relationships with other men. The history of 'Equity' reveals that appeals against the Royal Judges were made directly to the king who was known as the 'Fountain of Justice,' and often such appeals were considered on moral rights or natural justice. So, Equity or Natural Justice was established as it was less formal and technical than Common Law. The notion of rights appertaining to the individual person can be seen to have emerged from the dispute over Equity. It has been argued that rights would be unnecessary if there existed a rational social system.

Professor **DD Raphael** indicated that the primary function of the modern State is the keeping of order and the maintenance of security. It has often been said that the primary purpose of the State is to preserve 'law and order.' Ulster is the perfect example where 'law and order' has an authoritative role. There can be no social control without law and order and violence, or organised violence, is the ultimate weapon of any political order. For some cryptic reason, the authorities seldom consider 'justice and harmony' as a means to achieve order.

The long tragedy in Ireland can be traced back to 1920 when **Lloyd George** offered only Home Rule under the 'Government of Ireland Act.' Without doubt, the Act was provocative as it required Ireland to accept less than Canada had gained in 1867. It restricted government to only a limited number of matters and the right to continue electing MPs to Westminster. Moreover, Ireland was partitioned, with Home Rule in Ulster at Belfast and Home Rule in Eire at Dublin. Now, this is the crux of the problem and it reveals a fatal flaw in the democratic process. The Protestants would not accept being ruled by the Catholics, yet the Protestants comprised only 25% of Ireland's population. There was no talk of a referendum in those days. Today, the Protestants comprise 70% of the population of Northern Ireland. Sinn Fein rejected the Act. During the Falklands War, there was incessant propaganda about the right to self-determination and this is the IRA argument justifying their 'just war.' This is the democratic defect; when considering only Northern Ireland, the Protestants have a built-in majority; when considering the possibility of a United Ireland, the Catholics have a built-in majority. The problem is divergent; it cannot be solved; it can only be transcended. First, it must be recognised that a blunder was made in 1920; it must also be recognised that to participate in an election is implicitly to agree to the majority verdict; the government at Westminster must stop dithering and vacillating.

Power relates to ability, and in a social context, it means the ability to make people act in the way one wants them to act. To have authority to act is to have the right to act. The government exercising the role of authority have a duty to pursue justice in playing that role.

Professor Raphael asserted: 'The primary function of the State…in a negative function…it is the prevention of harm to existing rights or existing well-being, as contrasted with a positive function of adding to well-being or of adding new rights or redistributing old ones.'

Decisions by the people relate to democracy and decisions by the wise relate to goodness. The last two decades have destroyed the myth that good government is democratic government. History reveals that the rule of the majority often leads to unwise decisions, such as the imposition of the poll tax and the abolition of wage councils. We need a constraint to help those who are vulnerable to the excesses of centralised power. The rule of the majority is quite often oppressive, therefore, a 'Bill of Rights' is a constraint to counteract the excesses of centralised power. Democratic theories of government are based on the model below:

	INPUTS		OUTPUTS
	Social System	**Government**	**Policy Decision**

The social system is the pre-requisite for any government to make policy decisions. No society can exist without some form of social control. Now, our social system inevitably entails our cultural system. What is culture? The definition of culture has implied the contrast between animal nature and human nature; however, the psychology of culture relates to the human intellect and will to direct our actions.

A significant text on the 'Theory of Culture,' is the critical analysis made by **AL Kroeber and Clyde Kluckhohn** of several hundred definitions of culture. They arrived at this summary which they believed would be acceptable to all social scientists. 'Culture consists of morally correct behaviour acquired and transmitted by symbols, showing the way we live. The essence of culture is derived from traditional ideas that is the necessity of values. Culture systems, maybe considered as the results of human thought and action, as well as the guide for further action.' The question arises—can there be a stable society without a minimum of absolute values?

Talcott Parsons has been a leading character in social-scientific disciplines and his work has received widespread acclamation. Parsons's social 'theory of action' involves four action systems:

(i)   the social system,
(ii)   the personality system,
(iii)   the cultural system, and
(iv)   the organic system.

He defined the social system as a group of interacting persons incited to action by a tendency towards the 'optimisation of gratification' and dependent upon the situation, implicating relationships with others, is made compatible by a 'system of culturally constructed symbols.' The four active systems relate to end attainment, motivation, symbolisation, and adaptation. Any social system entails the interaction and interrelationships of human beings and the 'cultural system' is the key to pattern maintenance; in other words, the maintenance of the values truth, beauty and goodness as well as other values. In all social systems, there exists controversy on the best way to act, so there is a degree of tension in the system. Without this degree of tension, there would be no social change.

Unlike any structure in engineering where different types of force exist, a social system cannot achieve stable equilibrium. Equilibrium is most often affected by changes in the economy, or the destruction of the environment or by the addition of new laws, or by the subtraction of public assets. Equilibrium is also affected by cultural challenges such as the 'theory of evolution.' Society must be protected from destruction by the breaking stress of change. The prime function of the social system is the creation and maintenance of social order. Many believe that above the cultural system exists the sphere of 'ultimate reality' and the philosophy of materialism.

Karl Marx believed that all social change relates to the economy whereas Parsons believed that it relates to the 'value system.' The major fact derived from any sociological theory is that there is a dimension of determinism in any social change. It appears that man does not control his own destiny, so is there a supreme intelligence behind our 'value-system.'

Clifford Hill wrote, 'With no certain basis to the values of society and an ever-increasing rate of change in the normative structure and in social organisation, chaos is inevitable and the end result in terms of mounting chaos, normative anarchy, the breakdown of social organisation and the final disintegration of the entire system is equally inevitable.'

Can it be disputed that there is scant stability in society today? The essence of the culture system is derived from traditional ideas and especially their values which are related to virtues. It cannot be denied that in Britain, over the last four decades, rapid change has occurred. There has been an escape from truth, and without truth, there can be no justice. When human beings do not accept that an intelligent life is better than a stupid life; that truth is preferable to falsehood; that virtue is preferable to vice, then they are beyond the scope of rational persuasion and must be labelled abnormal, irrational.

Primarily, a social scientist is keenly interested in the actions of human beings and their reactions to predicaments which may or may not involve their institutions. **Jean-Paul Sartre** identified a serious predicament of human beings, namely, we are 'condemned to freedom.' When a human being acts his or her role, and then makes the excuse that I am only doing my job, then that human being lives in 'bad faith' Human beings cannot evade responsibility for their actions. Men live in 'bad faith' when they pretend that an action is necessary when in fact, they have the freedom of choice. When they reject this freedom, it is a refusal to face the struggle of choice.

Peter L Berger expressed it so completely: 'Capital punishment can serve as the paradigm for the combination of 'bad faith' with inhumanity, for each step of this monstrous process, as it is still practised in America, is an act of 'bad faith,' in which socially constructed roles are taken as alibis for personal cowardice and cruelty. The prosecuting attorney claims to suppress his sympathy to carry out his stern duty, as does the jury and the judge. Within the drama of a courtroom in which a capital case is tried, every one of those who prepare the eventual execution of the defendant is engaged in an act of deception—the deception that he is not acting as an individual, but only *qua* the role assigned to him in the edifice of legal fiction…The excuse of such men that they 'have no choice' is the fundamental lie on which all 'bad faith' rests.'

Society has different institutions which underpin the two major institutions, the family and the government; all rest on a non-material base. The following table is self-explanatory:

SOCIAL ORDER
GOVERNMENT Law, Taxes, Health, Well-Being, **FAMILY**

COMPONENTS of the **SOCIAL SYSTEM**	RELATING to the **COMPONENTS**
Education	Instruction
Architecture	Buildings
Agriculture	Land
Engineering	Machinery
Economics	Money
Ethics	Actions
Psychology	Behaviour
Biology	Life
Science	Method
Philosophy	Logic
Mathematics	Symbols
Art	Technique

History	Past Events
Naturalism	Material World
Religion	Spiritual World

BELIEFS   **VALUES**   **CULTURES**

There is a sociological maxim that where one social institution is subject to fundamental change, then others cannot remain isolated. The classic case has been the increase in one-parent families where the freedom to separate or the easier route to divorce affects moral values; it draws attention to a current social and political problem, namely, the evasion of responsibility. Of course, dependent upon the type of social change, there exists a strong possibility of the subsidence of the social base.

One of the greatest, if not the greatest political philosopher of the twentieth century was **Karl Popper.** He conceived society with a multitude of problems; therefore, he preferred societies which have a propensity to problem-solving. He thought that possible solutions could be submitted, examined and criticised, then either rejected or subjected to error elimination and improvement.

Karl **Popper,** the political philosopher in his two volumes of 'The Open Society and its Enemies,' highlighted the paradox of economic freedom where the powerful dominate the poor and he insisted we must construct social institutions, enforced by the power of the state, for the economically weak against the economically strong. We must demand that unrestrained capitalism gives way to economic interventionism. He argued that economic freedom ends in self-contradiction and he challenged: 'Which freedom should the state protect? The freedom of the labour market, or the freedom of the poor to unite? Whichever decision is taken, it leads to state intervention, to the use of organised political power, of the state as well as the unions, in the field of economic conditions…it is most important to realise that without a carefully protected free market, the whole economic system must cease to serve its only rational purpose, that is, *to satisfy the demands of the consumer.'*

Karl Popper submitted a key principle for society and the way that a government should direct policy, **Reduce to the minimum avoidable suffering.** This is not just a revision of the Utilitarian principle, 'Maximise happiness,' for it is impossible to know what makes everyone happy (do you make the rich happy by raising taxes?) However, it is possible to reduce human suffering. **Popper** wrote, '…there is, from the ethical point of view, no symmetry between suffering and happiness….human suffering makes a direct appeal, namely, the appeal for help, while there is no similar call to increase the happiness of a man who is doing well anyway. 'Maximise pleasure' is that it assumes in principle, a continuous pleasure-path scale which allows us to treat degrees of pain as negative degrees of pleasure. But, from the moral point of view, pain cannot be outweighed by pleasure, and especially, not one man's by another man's pleasure. Instead of the greatest happiness for the greatest number, one should demand, more modestly, the least amount of avoidable suffering for all.'

Popper's principle would undoubtedly lead to the elimination of many injustices, but how would this help to further the dictum, 'Find your relaxation in the arts.' So, we cannot escape from the two significant questions in political philosophy, 'What is the ultimate justification for the existence of any kind of government?' and 'Who should rule?' In answer to the first question; to help to promote conditions and circumstances, so that all citizens can pursue the 'good life' in what Popper called the 'Open Society.' Popper asserted, *all theories of sovereignty are paradoxical.* Who should rule? A dictator, the monarch, plutocrats, the proletariat, the majority party, or the philosopher-king. The question leads to the paradox identified by Popper. If power is offered to the wise man, then his wisdom will guide him: 'Not I but the morally good should be the ruler.' If power is offered to the morally good, then the response is likely to be: 'It is wrong for me to impose my will upon others. Not I but the majority should rule.' However, due to defects in the democratic system, the majority may argue: 'We need an ideal perfect man to bring about social justice and give us moral leadership.' Popper suggested that the question should be changed from 'Who should rule?' to 'How can the citizens prevent incompetent rulers from doing too much damage?'

Chapter 7
Economics and Extravagance

This chapter could well be extended to complete the book but it would then be inconsistent with the title, so brevity in some parts is essential. Economics is a subject inclined to be treated with disdain by some profound thinkers by reason of the economists' untested hypotheses and lack of consensus in their conclusions. The crystal balls of most economists are obscured because of their refusal to study *meta-economics.*

The influential word 'economics' is derived from the Greek word *oikonomia,* and it means a steward or a house (an asset) manager. It is opportune to raise two questions relating to its meaning:

(i)   Have human beings no responsibility for the planet Earth? and
(ii)   How are human beings managing the resources of the Earth?

Their progress in the management of resources leads to the question—is progress in economic theory possible?

Economics, like culture, involves human behaviour; it is the study of human behaviour in the relationships between human needs and desires, observing how they are or could be satisfied. Satisfaction is obtained by the procurement of goods or via personal or commercial services, such as the dairy that supplies the milk or the plumber who frees the frozen pipe. Relating to goods and services are the three 'factors of production,' land, labour and capital, but it applies to all the resources provided by nature; mineral resources, natural gas, fossil fuels, timber from forests, fish from the seas and energy from the wind and sun. Labour equates to human resources implicating the physical skills and mental abilities of people in all lands. In the course of all the productive operations, specialists in organisation and management techniques are required. Capital equates to fixed assets plus current assets less current liabilities; these include factories, offices, shops, power stations and many other kinds of factor capital such as plant, machinery, motor vehicles, office equipment, stocks of raw materials and work-in-progress, not forgetting cash in hand or at bank and sundry debtors.

At the end of production, the goods are transported to various places, home and possibly overseas and then they are usually sold to consumers. The goods such as bread are consumed and white goods have a limited usefulness; car insurance and the road fund licence reach a date of expiry, so the human needs remain and the cycle of activity continues as illustrated.

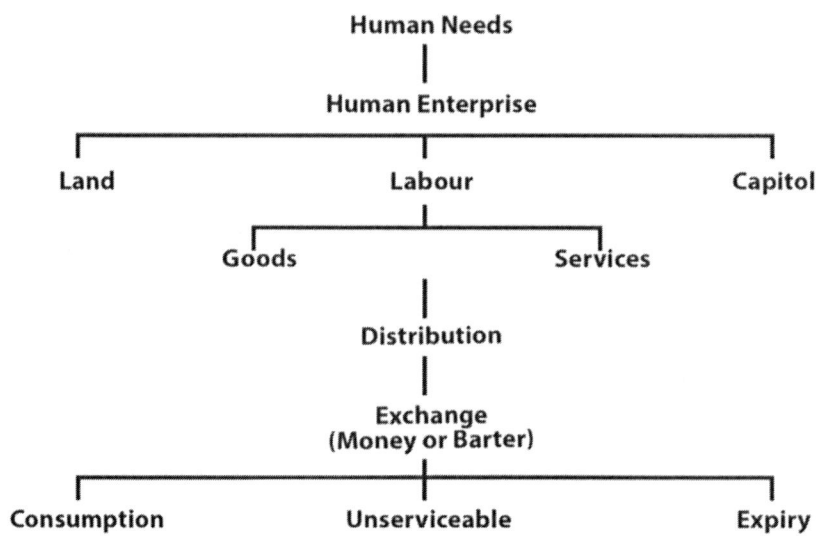

Two important concepts in economics are money and cost. Money is primarily a means of exchange; it is also a standard and store of value. Money is significant in accounts where records are made relating to deferred payments to creditors or by debtors. Money is also collected by governments via taxes in exchange for defence arrangements, health and education services, social security and other public services. Human needs entail everyone taking part in the cycle of activity. The factors of production are put into operation and rewards in the form of money are received. The reward to land is rent; the reward to labour is wages or salaries (the same thing except for status); the reward to capital is either interest or profit, sometimes both. In 'Small is Beautiful,' **Dr EF Schumacher** argued that the pursuit of profit has resulted in irrational planning, extreme economic inefficiency, disastrous environmental planning and inhumane working practices. Professor **James Meade** as well as **John Kenneth Galbraith** both recognised the existing injustice with respect to the distribution of wealth. Finally, a former professor of economics at Cambridge University, **Joan Robinson** wrote in her fine work, 'Freedom and Necessity,' this valid criticism of capitalism: 'Looking out upon this menacing scene, the apologists for modern capitalism have lost their self-confidence. They can find nothing better to offer than the doctrine of the lesser evil. To defend the bad against the worse is no inspiration to generous youth.'

Returning to the money concept, **Dr Schumacher** wrote, 'But what does it mean when we say that something is uneconomic? I am not asking what most people mean when they say this. They simply mean that it is like an illness; you are better off without it. No, I am asking, *what sort of meaning the method of economics actually produces.* And the answer to this question cannot be in doubt; something is uneconomic when it fails to earn an adequate profit in money terms. The method of economics does not and cannot, produce any other meaning. Numerous attempts have been made to obscure this fact, and they have caused a great deal of confusion, but the fact remains.'

Traditional wisdom insisted that money is the 'root of all evil.' Contemporary wisdom insists that the 'lack of money is the root of all evil.' Neither assertion is entirely true, only partly true. In 1980, a poll was taken in Japan and 60% of those interviewed believed that 'money is almighty.' The wisdom of Solomon is paraphrased: 'If thou sees the oppression of the poor, and violent perverting of justice anywhere, marvel not about the matter; the profit of the earth is for all. He that loveth money will not be satisfied with money, neither any lover of wealth will increase; this is just vanity.' It remains true, an extreme desire for money motivates a human being to lie, cheat and pervert justice.

In economic theory, models have been introduced; a model may be defined as a set of entities in a system, namely, the concepts and equations of an economic system, and their relations in the system, especially with the role-actors.

From an empirical standpoint, it has been suggested that there is a need for four types of models.

(i) A master model of the economy.

(ii) A market model indicating the changes in the amount of sales and purchases and the anticipated trading prices.

(iii) A motion model for estimating the rate of increase or decrease in growth.

(iv) A mirror model for reflecting the vicissitudes dictated by the global economy.

Most laymen are aware of the three elements required to produce goods, but maybe they are not **aware** of the possible combinations available to produce different types and quantities of goods and services. The factors of production are resources which can be in short supply at any point in time. It has been stated so often by many economists that *resource allocation* remains the central economic problem.

How the factors of production are used depends upon decisions made by individuals and authorities? Land can be used to grow any one of a variety of crops; or it can be sown as a permanent pasture for livestock to graze; or it can be planted with saplings for long-term timber production; or it can be landscaped and transformed into a green **park;** or it can be developed into a golf course; or it can have the topsoil removed for concrete to be laid to construct a car **park;** or it can be used as a site for a supermarket, shopping complex, factory, warehouse, offices or houses; or it can be used for the building of airports, motorways and other roads. Also, land can be used for all the leisure facilities, swimming pools, cricket, football, rugby and hockey pitches, tennis courts, race courses, athletic stadiums, theatres and cinemas.

The greater amount of resources used in the production of weapon systems, building nuclear power stations and motorway constructions, the smaller the amount of resources available for the building of homes, hospitals and schools. The logic of production and consumption is neither the logic of nature nor that of a rational society. The allocation of finite resources cannot satisfy unlimited consumer desires. Priorities must be established to solve the economic absurdity, but such actions cause political and social tension. Freedom of choice has become a dogma to such an extent that many human beings are prepared to suffer ill-health rather than change their existing lifestyle. Besides a biological problem, here is an acute psychological problem.

It is relevant to quote a philosophical gem submitted by **Arthur Schopenhauer.** What is the nature of human beings? Why? To be creatures of want, need and desire. Needing and desiring is our natural condition, and since need is unpleasant, it urges us to take steps to satisfy it. When we satisfy a need, we experience pleasure, but only for a short interval, for once the need is satisfied, the condition on which the pleasure depended no longer exists. Further, since needing and desiring is our natural condition, the satisfied need will be almost immediately replaced by a non-satisfied need. So, while the needs of human beings are continuous and inevitable, the pleasure of satisfying their need is uncertain.

Gandhi pointed out, 'Earth provides enough to satisfy every man's need, but not for every man's greed.' Contemporary economics includes the proposition that increasing consumption is necessary to maintain economic growth. For economists, the highest of all values is economic growth, so temperance is an obstruction to their goal. This is the question to be answered—can it be denied that there is a limit to economic growth? If economic growth is the goal for the most prosperous nations, then it must be the goal for the third world nations and hardwood forests are a lucrative means to income or to reduce debt, irrespective of the consequences of adding further stress to the environment.

Unlimited economic growth or the production of more and more goods with no relation to human needs is the logic of the lunatic. The deliberate extension of human needs and desires is not only irrational, it is having a disastrous effect upon the environment and the social structure. As economic growth improves the standard of living it also worsens the quality of human life. In our mobile mad, space stripping, misused energy, wanton waste society the 'Law of Disequilibrium' rules.

Authoritarian systems control the production and supply of goods and services that is assumed to satisfy consumers' needs. Such a system works effectively in a small simple economy.

The existing economic system, the Market Economy, arranges the allocation of resources via the business enterprises whose materials, labour, overheads and profit calculations establish the price mechanism, so providing consumers with access to resources. A concourse of buyers and sellers represents a market. In the market system, no distinction is made between those transactions which produce maximum benefit to the economy and those that contribute minimum benefit. Of course, there is a valid distinction between the transactions, although the totals of the transactions may be identical. The following classic case displays one of the absurdities of the market system. The owner of a small business decided to put his exceptional property on the market. So, he engaged the services of an estate agent who valued the property at £400,000, and informed the seller that the commission payable would be 2% of the contract price plus VAT. A buyer emerged in less than seven days and declined to haggle about the agent's price as the frontage of the property was long enough for two building plots although planning consent had to be obtained. During the same week, the proprietor of the small business ordered four wood-working machines; a spindle moulder, a band saw, a cross-cutting saw and a hollow chisel mortising machine. The capital equipment was needed to increase the production of reproduction furniture sold in the Japanese market. The cost of the fixed assets came to just short of £8,000 and the estate agent's commission amounted to £8,000. The owner of the small business concluded that although both transactions were legitimate, one was clearly legitimate robbery.

Whether the conclusion is valid, it is a subject of controversy. Nevertheless, when considering the purchase of the capital goods, there was a series of transactions prior to the purchase, and the operation of the machines produced a further series of transactions. The market is composed of institutions in which individualism is the object of worship. A purchaser has no responsibility apart from ensuring that the goods bought are not stolen. Buyers have no responsibility to buy home-produced goods rather than imported goods, even though their actions can have an adverse effect on the balance of payments. If business organisations are not competitive, then surgery is performed on the fixed and variable costs, which invariably means the disposal of human assets although they were depreciated to zero value anyway.

John Maynard Keynes in his 'Essays on Persuasion,' was prompted to ponder about the 'Economic Possibilities for our Grandchildren.' he thought that the economic problem would be finally solved: 'Now it is true that the needs of human beings may seem to be insatiable. But they fall into two classes—those needs which are absolute in the sense that we feel them whatever the situation of our fellow human beings may be, and those which are relative in the sense that we feel them only if their satisfaction lifts us above, makes us feel superior to our fellows…a point may soon be reached, much sooner perhaps than we are all of us aware of, when these needs are satisfied in the sense that we prefer to devote our further energies to non-economic purposes.'

'I see us free therefore, to return to some of the most sure and certain principles of religion and traditional virtue—that avarice is a vice, that the exaction of usury is a misdemeanour, and the love of money is detestable, that those walk most truly in the paths of virtue and sane wisdom who take least thought for tomorrow. We shall once more value ends above means and prefer the good to the useful. We shall honour those who can teach us how to pluck the hour and the day virtuously and well, the delightful people who are capable of taking direct enjoyment in things, the lilies of the field who toil not, neither do they spin. For only they can lead us out of the tunnel of economic necessity into daylight.'

He issued this warning, 'Beware! The time for all this is not yet. For at least another hundred years, we must pretend to ourselves and to everyone that **fair is foul** and **foul is fair;** for foul is useful and fair is not. Avarice, usury and precaution must be our Gods for a little longer still.'

Such a futile warning overlooked the traditional wisdom, 'Whatsoever thou soweth thou shalt reap.' Seventy years have elapsed since the warning was proclaimed yet society is still in the tunnel. During this period, a colossal quantity of the earth's capital has been squandered and pollution costs have rocketed into the biosphere. The confusion of fair and foul in the market system has penetrated into the social system. It has been suggested that **Keynes** was the saviour of the capitalist system by condemning governments for not using their spending power to reduce unemployment to a minimum level. The Keynesian revolution certainly made an impact upon economic theory although today the doctrine has been distorted. Demand management is used to deflate the volume of output by tacitly increasing unemployment to affect an improvement in the balance of payments as well as to cure an inflation ill.

Despite his preposterous proposition, 'fair is not useful,' but 'foul is useful,' Keynes deserves praise for wrestling with the problem of mass unemployment existing between the two wars. Whether economics is a science or sophistry, only time will tell, but Keynes was aware of the magnetic attraction of economic topics when he wrote, 'Practical men who believe themselves quite exempt from any intellectual influences are usually the slaves of some defunct economist.' Practical men ought to be interested in *meta-economics.*

The predicament of British industry at the end of the seventies was in some way similar to the predicament of the coal industry in 1926. To maintain competitiveness, the coal owners were compelled to decrease their costs so as to remain viable. The mine owners demanded a reduction in the wages of miners and also an extension of the working hours. The miners retorted, 'Not a penny off our pay, not a minute on the day.' This historical event reveals the core of the economic problem. Such a confrontation is rare today as industrial workers have become property owners and motivation by fear remains covert policy, so in order to keep wages at a low-level, redundancies are kept high.

Unemployment in the eighties was comparable to the levels that dismayed **Keynes**, but it must be pointed out that the population has considerably increased. It is interesting to trace how Keynesian economic models came to dominate in the early post-war years. The relation between total demand and level of unemployment is a central factor in Keynesian economic theory.

In the House of Commons, soon after the Normandy Invasion in 1944, **Ernest Bevin** gave an account of a visit he made to Portsmouth on 4 June prior to the invasion. His companion was **Winston Churchill** and together they passed between a body of troops who were selected to spearhead the invasion. This question was put to Bevin, "Ernie, when we have done this job for you, are we going back on the dole?" Both Churchill and Bevin responded, "No, you are not."

Their response was predetermined for approximately three weeks prior to D-Day, the war cabinet had considered and approved the white paper on unemployment policy. The influence of Keynes's economic theory was implicit in this unprecedented declaration, 'The Government accept as one of their primary aims and responsibilities the maintenance of a high and stable level of employment after the **war.**' The prospect of stabilising demand at a high level caused an outbreak of insomnia at the Treasury.

Post-war governments economic objectives were fourfold:

(i) Stabilisation of a high level of employment.
(ii) Stabilisation of prices.
(iii) Stabilisation of the balance of payments.
(iv) Speedy rate of growth.

In his 'General Theory of Employment, Interest and Money,' **Keynes** showed a remarkable understanding of financial and business conduct. **Keynes** recognised that there are three key sets of expenditure dependent mainly upon the quantity of national income. The simple equation is $Y = I + C + (G - T)$ where:

Y= Income

I=Investment

C=Consumption

G=Government Expenditure

T=Taxation

Income=Investment Expenditure + Consumption Expenditure + Government Expenditure

An important factor not taken into account in the equation is the quantity obtained from all individual incomes that are not contained in consumption expenditure, namely savings, **Keynes** considered savings as 'a mere residual.'

Consumption is a set proportion (c) of income, that is, C=c Y

Keynes conceived a 'fundamental psychological law,' which claims that 'men are disposed as a rule and on the average, to increase their consumption as their income increases, but not as much as the increase in income.' Reflecting upon the existing global debt situation and the popular philosophy, 'live now, pay later,' this psychological law applies to some. From **Keynes's** conception, it is obvious that c will be less than one and more than zero. So, the equation is transformed to:

$$Y = \frac{1}{1-c} (I + (G-T))$$

The coefficient $1/(1 - c)$ is the Keynesian *multiplier* which Keynes estimated would be a constant of around two. With a coefficient of two, the combined increase in investment and government expenditure would produce an increase in income of about twice that amount. It can be seen that savings and investment schemes have a direct effect on the amount of unemployment. Despite Keynesian economic theory solving the post-war employment problem, the limitations of the theory were exposed when dealing with the problem of regional unemployment. Due to the lack of skilled workers and essential resources, there is no incentive to invest in poverty-stricken areas; there is a supply failure.

Before considering the 'Classical Theory' which **Keynes** opposed, it is necessary to emphasise the meaning of the concepts, demand and supply. The demand for any goods and services at an offered price is related to how much can be purchased per unit of time at that price. Therefore, in economic theory, time is money when related to wages per hour.

The supply of goods or services is related to how much is offered per unit of time. In this sense, supply means without exception, supply at a price. Changes in demand and supply have an impact upon costs and wage costs are an integral part of the price system. Wage and price levels interact which can lead to an increase or a decrease in unemployment. Of course, money relates to the price level, or more precisely, the quantity of money and the demand for money for investment implicates the supply of money for investment dependent upon society's inclination to save. Therefore, the foremost market relationship is between the demand for money and the supply of money. Presuming increased savings occur from increased income, then another relationship emerges and the rate of interest is another significant factor.

Economists of the 'Classical' school assert that the state of demand and supply in the labour market decides the level of unemployment. The demand for labour and the supply of labour available for employment at a set wage rate ought to produce an equilibrium wage rate. Therefore, with the existence of an 'equilibrium' wage level, there would be job opportunities for workers offering their services. Hence, it was asserted that severe unemployment was the result of the standard wage level being too high. The 'Classical' school's solution=cut wages, cut unemployment. Such a solution ignores the consequences that emerge whereby there is no escape from the poverty trap, even with the assistance of income support. It must be repeated, there can be no strong democracy without the twin pillars of liberty and equality being favoured alike.

Adam Smith revealed in his *Wealth of Nations* that the wages of the majority of citizens were inadequate to satisfy the basic needs of the family. He claimed that wages were subject to control by infant mortality; when conditions improved to decrease infant mortality, then wages would decrease. When infant mortality increased again to its appropriate figure, then wages would re-adjust. Smith failed to condemn this deplorable situation or to recommend any social reforms. Adam Smith's book is lacking in both rational and moral conviction, hence his book tends to confuse rather than convey the fact that free market forces cause much harm as well as good. He ignored the fact that equity equates to social justice.

When it is reported that a few managing directors receive an annual income of £1,000,000 whilst the average employee of their group of companies receives

£12,000 per annum, then the managing director must be identified with the image of God. Of course, those of the *laissez faire* school claim it is just part of the price mechanism operating in a free market. This is the question they refuse to answer—is such gross inequality in income distribution morally justifiable? The gap between rich and poor can never decline unless attention is paid to incomes.

Not too long ago, there was much discussion about the absurd notions of two groups who were politically poles apart; the National Front and the Militant Tendency. They were labelled extremists, yet the notion that an income differential of more than 20:1 is not extreme is the absurdity of all absurdities. It has been suggested that culture may be harmed by too much equality, but in a world of such obscene inequalities in income distribution, there can be no danger to our culture from equality but certainly from injustice.

The writer cannot accept the bare creed of **Robert Green Ingersoll,** 'Justice is the only worship,' but he agrees that justice ought to be pursued steadfastly. When educated human beings argue that the council tax which replaced the iniquitous poll tax system is a just method for producing local government revenue, then there is something fundamentally wrong with our education system. When politicians argue that greater equality is gradually occurring through changes in our taxation system by accepting an upper tax rate limit of 40%, then there is something wrong with our political system. Prudence has a far different meaning than that used by politicians; the pursuit of the 'public good' must involve actions that lessen the problems relating to our bio-physical and socio-cultural environment.

Most economists view Satan as inflation in the price system which they argue is due to excessive wage increases. Professor **W Phillips** developed the 'Phillips Curve' by plotting the percentage level of unemployment, the independent variable, with the annual percentage rate of wage increases, the dependent variable. He discovered that a bargain was struck between low inflation and level of employment. However, it was observed that by deliberately increasing unemployment, the power of the trade unions as well as excess demand could be reduced; wage rates would tend to stabilise so that *cost-inflation* would return to a reasonable level. The activities of trade unions in wage-bargaining is group selfishness, but then the activities of the Confederation of British Industry and the Institute of Directors are far from altruistic. Government composed of individuals with prejudiced ideas (not wise ideas) is also another form of group selfishness because the political and economic system demands such an attitude.

The existing predicament prevails because the *laissez faire* supporters appear to have the upper hand, namely, market forces must be subject to minimum control. The critics know that the distribution of income and wealth is a denial of justice, but to speak about increases in taxation is an electoral liability. For a long period in the past, such a declaration would have been labelled as **Marxist** propaganda instead of a critique of capitalism; John Kenneth Galbraith broke the taboo:

> The *formal* liberal attitude towards inequality has changed little over the years. The Liberal has partly accepted the view of the well-to-do that it is a trifle uncouth to urge a policy of soaking the rich. Yet on the whole, the rich man remains the antagonist of the poor. Economic legislation, above all tax policy, continues to be a contest, however unequal, between the interests of the two. No other question in economic policy is ever so important as the effect of a measure on the distribution of income. The test of the good liberal is still that he is never fooled, that he never yields on issues favouring the rich.

At some future date, the distribution of income and wealth will have to be addressed for the global environment problem implicates poverty. The problem that must be addressed is—why is there such extreme inequality in income and wealth distribution? When there is a demand for a certain ability, then there is an appropriate payment for that ability dictated by the market. Few would deny that a doctor or a dentist deserve a greater income than a docker or a lorry driver. Those who have the physical ability to undertake manual work tend to be in excess supply, whereas those with exceptional mental ability tend to be in short supply. When there is a great demand for an ability in short supply, then the possessor of that ability can receive an income known in economic jargon as 'rent of ability.' Obviously, inequality in income is unavoidable and necessary for the proper function of the market system. When sportsmen and entertainers who are non-productive receive incomes in the region of £10 to the power of 6, whereas a skilled worker may receive an income in the region of £10 to the power of 4, then there is something manifestly foul to use the language of Keynes. Anyone who knows anything about the subject accepts that job evaluation is a first priority in any income policy.

The problem cannot be solved; it can be only transcended when a government finds the courage to accept the responsibility for fixing income differentials. In dividing the economic cake, by what ratio should the largest portion be cut to the smallest portion, and who ought to receive the largest portion? Such an exercise involves making value judgements which are outside the scope of economic theory. Philosophy commenced with the value judgement—an intelligent life is more desirable than a foolish life.

Professor **James Meade** revealed the 'fantastic' inequalities with respect to the distribution of wealth in his excellent book, 'Efficiency, Equality and the Ownership of Capital.' How has such extreme inequality evolved? Let us consider a society in which citizens have no wealth and all citizens receive the same income. The professor analysed the links in the chain of the acquisition of wealth.

Link 1. Ability is a poor man's wealth which predetermines the introduction of income differentials. Inequality in wealth arises because those with higher incomes can increase their savings at a faster rate than those with lower incomes. Also, older persons have had a longer period to increase their wealth than younger persons.

Link 2. Social circumstances are significant whereby marriage contracts are made between partners having a concord of intelligence; therefore, both receive similar incomes. Genetic circumstances are also significant; exceptionally intelligent parents produce children as intelligent as themselves. Without doubt, intelligence is usually related to high income attainment.

Link 3. High savings associated with high incomes inevitably lead to the purchase of private property, and the rate of increase in price with respect to the function of time ensures that the asset does not depreciate, it tends to appreciate.

Link 4. The inheritance process gives the opportunity to those who inherit wealth to increase their wealth.

Link 5. Savings acquired from higher incomes plus social advantage gives the wealthy the means to arrange a better education for their children so that they can pursue a profession or a business career. The class system makes contacts between such classes essential so as to gain more wealth. By comparison, the poor receive a poor education so restricting their opportunity to secure a job or a higher income. Low income almost denies the satisfaction of basic needs; accordingly savings are non-existent. Usually, the temptation to borrow money causes a debt problem, consequently, the poor suffer psychologically as well as physically.

Link 6. Knowledge is wealth and wealth is power, so the rich are able to influence events by dominating the mass media and by maintaining the *status quo*. Lest it may be misconstrued, there is no direct action by the rich, but Professor Meade showed that once inequality exists, then market forces work in favour of the rich and against the poor. In any value system, equity must be present, so those who support the existing reality are prone to a false sense of values.

Many naive persons conceive wealth as only money, whereas the value of exchange accounts for only part of a business concern's assets. However, in any economic model, the money factor must be taken into account. Monetary policy, like all divergent problems attracts two points of view—the 'Keynesian' view and the 'Monetarist' view. The Keynesian model relates to interest-rate policy; in other words, the price of money and credit. Professor **M Friedman** was one of the leading proponents of 'Monetarist Theory,' and his basic belief was paradoxically simple but complex. The professor based his belief on the first market connection between the demand for money and the total supply of money. His theory treats inflation as a function of the total money supply, but its measurement is far from scientific.

The professor insisted that governments cause inflation by increasing the total supply of money by the printing press. The greater the amount of paper money printed, the smaller its value related to purchasing power. The Monetarist's sole policy instrument is to control the printing press which in turn controls the total supply of money. The steadfast policy is that for any slight increase in the total supply of money, there must be a corresponding increase in output. Unfortunately, although the policy is efficient in controlling the disease of inflation, there are painful repercussions in the manner of exceedingly high unemployment.

In 1983, the Bank of England Panel of Academic Consultants considered the UK aspects involved in the book by Milton Friedmanand Anna Schartz called, 'Monetary Trends in the United States and the United Kingdom.' They examined the statistical procedures used in the book, the historical evidence, and the extent to which the authors' conclusions were valid. Inevitably, it was a specialist's function which few laymen would understand, but the conclusion contained in their paper was far from difficult to understand.

The conclusion arrived at by **David F Hendry** and **Neil R Ericsson** is summarised: 'A number of assertions in Friedman and Schwartz concerning the validity of their money demand equation have been tested using their data series for the United Kingdom and were found to be without empirical support. Simply 'corroborating' a subset of the implications of a theory is not an adequate justification for deeming it useful…rigorous evaluation of empirical claims seems a necessary first step towards taking the **con** out of economics.'

The inequalities which clearly exist in the United Kingdom (Is it united?) are trivial compared to those that exist in the Third World. Poverty, disease, ignorance and gross inequality abound on an increasing scale where the sole growth rate is in population, which contributes to the increased demand for food, housing, health and education resources. A person has no need to study economics to come to the conclusion that there is something tragically wrong with the global economy.

Nearly all the Third World nations were the victims of colonial rule and it is only in the last fifty years that they have won their right to self-determination. For over 200 years, British Industry has developed to its present state of high technology along with other industrialised nations. The global economic system reveals a tremendous 'development gap' which in the free trade world will continue to widen because of the built-in advantage of the industrialised nations. Whilst most rich nations now live beyond their means, some poor nations cannot supply their citizens with the means to live.

America is assumed to be the richest western nation, yet in October 1990, the American President when referring to the national debt declared, there is 'a cancer gnawing away at our nation's health.' After 200 years, the American debt amounted to $1,000 billion; after five more years, the debt was doubled to $2,000 billion; after a further five years the national debt topped $3,000 billion; the amount to service the debt was estimated to be $260 billion in 1990 and $300 billion in 1996. Recalling the Greek word *oikonomos,* it is divided into two parts; the first part *oiko* meaning a house; the second part *nomos* meaning a manager. America is managing its house awfully and the question is—how much longer will the rest of the world continue to finance this mountain of debt? The unpalatable truth is that at some future date, taxes will have to be increased considerably but politicians know that this is an electoral liability.

When attention is focused on the UK public finances, within a short time, credibility is stretched to the elastic limit. The breaking point of disbelief is reached when an analysis is made of the public finances between 1974 and 1994. This period has been selected for it includes the management of State affairs by different political parties. The previous government boasted that it could manage the economy much better than the existing government. Is this true? The existing government is accused of being prone to high spending, yet when examining the national debt in 1979 and the amount in 1994, the previous government may be accused of managing the economy badly. When public income and expenditure are examined over this period, then alarm bells ought to be sounding. The UK is amassing a national debt not on the scale of the United States, but the future generations will have to suffer the consequences.

Before concentrating attention on public accounts and fiscal measures, it is appropriate to consider the balance of payments implicating exchange rates. The meaning of the balance of payments relates to one of three possible conditions. The first is self-explanatory; exports equals imports. When this condition is not achieved, then *disequilibrium* exists. When the monetary measure of a nation's exports exceeds the monetary measure of its imports, its balance of trade is deemed to be auspicious or favourable. When the reverse condition comes into existence, then the nation's balance of trade is deemed to be adverse or unfavourable. Of course, the balance of payments will always be balanced since any shortfall in the current account is rectified by a transfer from the capital account; added to the credits and exports of the account is the sum from reserves and foreign borrowings.

Since 1945, the **UK** has frequently suffered a balance of payments problem, in other words, an unfavourable balance. The method to eliminate the *disequilibrium* in the balance of payments is to decrease the cost of our exports and increase the cost of our imports. The usual cry is that we must become more competitive; to become more competitive the advice was that we must become leaner and fitter. So, factor costs must be reduced to the minimum, that is, wages, salaries, rents and interest. At the same time, output must be increased. This has been the method mainly used since 1979 which has resulted in higher levels of unemployment.

The 'devaluation method' has been used by the **UK** in an attempt to correct its balance of payments problem. In the first post-war years, the exchange rate between the pound and the dollar approximated to this equation: £1=$4. In colloquial terms, one dollar was equivalent to five bob. In 1948, the government was forced to devalue the pound and the exchange rate equation changed to £1=$2.80. In 1964, the Labour government inherited a severe balance of payments problem after 13 years of 'never had it so good' economic policy.

Hence, in 1967, the pound was devalued again by 14%; the equation then became £1=$2.40. The improvement in the balance of payments from 1967 to 1971 has been recorded as a remarkable success for the devaluation exercise although other factors aided the success.

However, in 1972, a fresh crisis arose when cost-inflation appeared to be heading for heights unknown. In June 1972, currency speculators targeted the pound and the government appeared powerless as it watched the nation's reserves dwindle. The government was forced to allow the pound to float freely in the exchange rate market which was more or less pre-determined by the Smithsonian Agreement of November 1971. The agreement was put to the severe test in January 1974, when the Arab Organisation of Petroleum Exporting Countries dictated that the price of oil would be increased fourfold and as the **UK** was dependent on a large amount of imported oil, so the effect was devastating. The increased price of oil on top of the inflation pressures led to a current account deficit in 1974 of over £5,000 million. In 1976, the **UK** government was forced to go cap in hand to the IMF because its balance of payments was in 'fundamental disequilibrium.' During the past twenty years, the exchange rate has floated down to £1=$1.50, yet the UK still has a balance of payments problem. Devaluation used to be toxic to many past MPs, but now it is accepted as necessary medicine. Reality is the state of things, and the parlous state of the UK finance is a warning to expect trouble in the future. The warning is that rising national debt could lead the UK into severe social difficulties. This cannot be brushed aside as a pessimistic subjective opinion. The facts cannot be concealed; by the millennium, the UK national debt will be near to £400 billion; at an interest rate of 6%, the cost to service the debt equals £24 billion. One penny added to the standard tax rate yields a total of £1.5 billion; so just to service the debt would require an increase in the standard rate of tax from 23 pence in the pound to 39 pence in the pound on taxable income, yet the existing top rate of tax is only 40 pence in the pound. Those politicians who keep arguing for reductions in tax as an incentive to work harder and to increase consumer spending are out of touch with reality. Income tax rates have been slashed since 1979 which has reduced revenue from income tax leading to budget deficits devoid of prudence.

The budget is the means to manage the nation's house and like all households, it involves a source of income and the sum of expenditure. Any government is also concerned about revenue and expenditure, but the budget is also the means to control the economy to a great degree. The budget was believed to be a device to improve or preserve the general prosperity. This belief has been shaken as indirect taxes have been raised considerably. The increase in indirect taxes has not alleviated the problem; it has highlighted the problem. By increasing VAT to 17.5% and by imposing VAT on fuel and energy, it has once again raised the argument about indirect taxes.

Taxation is an anathema to the average person but without taxation, society would become a jungle; however, any person has a right to challenge his/her tax assessment providing that it is within the legal framework. Current self-assessment is not a means of evading tax. One of Adam Smith's 'Canons of Taxation' is that taxation should be equal or every person should pay the same proportion of their income. In the past, controversy has abounded with respect to the two types of taxation, direct taxation and indirect taxation.

To avoid this becoming a treatise on taxation, attention is focused on personal taxation. Adam Smith's canon for equal taxation conflicts with the principle of justice. First, the *per capita* tax, whereby equal means that everyone pays the same amount of tax _irrespective of the amount of their income. Second, the *proportional* tax, whereby equal means that all pay the same percentage of tax related to their income. Both forms of tax on incomes are regressive as the person on low income is penalised far greater than the person on high income. The fairest method of taxation is *Progressive* taxation, whereby equal means that everyone who receives a certain level of income will pay a certain percentage rate of tax up to a certain limit; everyone whose income is above that limit, then the excess of income will be subject to a higher percentage rate of tax. At the present time, there are two major rates of tax, namely, 20% and 40%.

Direct taxes also include corporation tax, capital gains tax, development gains tax and capital transfer tax. Direct taxes are the most equitable because they affect persons who have the means to pay them. To lessen the stark inequalities in the distribution of income and wealth, there is no better method than by *progressive* taxation. Indirect taxes are taxes that are not directed against a particular person but persons in general. Such taxes are purchase taxes, sales taxes, taxes on beer, wine and spirits, taxes on petrol and fuel oil, road fund tax, betting and gaming taxes and finally value added tax which replaced purchase tax. The latter tax is clearly regressive and it is identified with Adam Smith's canon; taxes should be equal. There are two justifiable criticisms of indirect taxation: (1) the manual worker and the millionaire both pay the same amount of tax on household goods; (2) impartiality cannot be achieved, for indirect taxes can be avoided by an individual who refuses to smoke, drink, gamble or own a motor car. These all relate to a poor man's luxuries, so he must either abstain or perhaps be influenced by temperance; indirect taxes do not worry a rich man. **John Kenneth Galbraith** highlighted the case against a certain indirect tax being used too lavishly.

There is another objection to greatly multiplied use of the sales tax (VAT) which is that, unlike the personal and corporation taxes, it makes no positive contribution to economic stability. The latter do so in two respects. Falling on the corporations and the well-to-do, they weigh most heavily on income that is on its way to be saved rather than on income that is on its way to be spent for consumer goods. The investment of saved income has long been considered the most mercurial and hence the least certain link between the receipt of income and its return to the spending stream. The income tax thus taps and ensures spending where this is intrinsically the least certain. Income taxes and especially the personal income tax have, in addition, their role as built-in stabilisers of the economy. The much-increased use of the sales tax…has long been the fond dream of conservatives.

A government has three options when preparing a budget. It can opt for a *neutral* budget whereby any tax changes do not alter either side of the receipts and expenditure account; it can opt for a budget *deficit* whereby the expenditure is far more than the receipts; or it can opt for a budget *surplus* whereby the receipts are far more than the expenditure. Of course, any chancellor reviews the state of the economy, then makes a decision as to whether there is a need for the encouragement of demand. High unemployment eventually prompts the chancellor to budget for a deficit by reducing taxation which he hopes will lead to higher spending.

At the beginning of the eighties and nineties, the UK experienced high levels of unemployment which has had a severe impact upon the social security budget. In 1984, the total expenditure on social security amounted to £38,908 million and by 1994, it had risen to £87,400 million. The consequences of such excessive expenditure caused a record budget deficit of £50,309 million in 1993, hence, from 1993 to 1994, the national debt interest increased from £19,189 million to £23,708 million.

Such figures stretch individual credibility to the limit. The £50 billion deficit incurring a £3.5 billion debt interest charge ought to have been a signal to raise direct taxes, not to reduce them and continue the sequence of budget deficits; at the same time, there can be no doubt that public expenditure should have been pruned severely. In 1988, because of the poverty trap, the government introduced the income support scheme. It now amounts to nearly one-fifth of the social security budget or over £16 billion. This is a direct subsidy to counter low pay. The social security budget accounts for approximately one-third of the national total expenditure. Besides the acceleration in the growth of income support, there has been a growth in housing benefit fraud. A 'Social Security Select Committee' discovered that some landlords draw over £1,000,000 a year in housing benefit fraud via their tenants. It was asserted by a prominent political leader that property is a good investment. For the older generation, this cannot be denied as the price of property has increased 3,000% in 40 years. However, many who were unfortunate to follow the investment advice shortly found that their mortgage was greater than the value of their property; they had not purchased a single brick; most suffered a period of anxiety.

Like all investments, there is a degree of risk involved for all markets fluctuate; although markets always seem to be rising, on occasions, there have been disastrous falls. The paradox remains—all nations require social stability, yet markets would not function if there was stability; gains and losses relate to the fluctuation in market prices. Increase in prices implicates the concept of inflation; the concept really relates to the differential calculus, namely, the increase in price with respect to the function of time. In other words, the consequences of inflation relate to how rapidly prices are increasing over a period of time. Since 1970, inflation has been a major problem of governments; by 1972, price increases resulted in an inflation rate of 10% and climbed to 26% in 1974. Economic history records that the State's financial matters were managed much better from 1945–70, compared to the succeeding twenty-five years. Is it wise to allow the State's debt to rise for political ends and how is this to be reconciled with the 'public good?'

When the proceeds of privatisation or the sale of national assets came to be recorded in the public accounts, the sums received were dealt with as negative expenditure. Consequently, the transactions were recorded in the current account, whereas in fact, it was a transaction relating to the national balance sheet. The government used the monies to supplement its income; this had been affected by its policy of considerably reducing income tax; rationally, the monies ought to have been used to reduce the national debt, not to reduce taxes. The nation's accounts were treated like Steptoe and Son's receipts and payments book; not only was it erroneous book-keeping but it was poor economic management. Also, no efficient business organisation sells off its indispensable assets at knock-down prices.

From 1979, UK citizens were subjected to perpetual propaganda against nationalised industries. Nationalisation was made to appear as a crime against society although some nationalised industries made remarkable achievements. In the 'Acquisitive Society,' **RH Tawney** indicated the real reason why nationalisation was rejected. 'The objection to public ownership, in so far as it is intelligent, is in reality an objection to over-centralisation. But the remedy for over-centralisation is not the maintenance of functionless property in private hands, but the *decentralised ownership of public property.* In a rational society, large-scale enterprises should never be in private ownership. Why?' RH Tawney gave this irrefutable reason: 'In large-scale enterprise, private ownership is a fiction for the purpose of enabling functionless owners to live parasitically on the labour of others. It is not only unjust but also an irrational element which distorts all relationships within the enterprise.' **Tawney** emphasised that the prime function of any nationalised industry must be to serve the public interest.

In recent years, the citizens of the United Kingdom have seen a complete rejection of public ownership and the complete acceptance of private ownership. It has revealed more than intellectual poverty but a richness in stupidity. In politics, there are two fanatical wings with respect to the ownership of property—one wing believes that all the industries should be privately owned; the other wing believes that all the industries should be in public ownership. **Harold Macmillan** thought it was absurd to put the 'family silver' up for sale or to dispose of the national assets; it can only be done once and it is difficult to retrieve the national assets.

Many pseudo-socialists in the New Labour Party are really converts to the capitalist system, thus they have no faith in nationalised industries. Because nationalisation policies are considered an electoral liability, they have been excluded from policy documents. For some cryptic reason, it is argued that private ownership aided by private greed will produce economic growth. In the controversial, 'Communist Manifesto,' **Karl Marx and Friedrich Engels** both recognised the inevitable consequences when the national assets are transferred to private ownership: 'The bourgeoisie, whenever it has got the upper hand, has put an end to all feudal, patriarchal, idyllic relations and has left no other nexus between man and man than *naked self-interest.'*

The New Labour Party made a tragic mistake when it voted to abolish Clause Four in its constitution; the disagreeable paragraph in the clause should have been amended. It is apposite to recall the key paragraph in Clause Four: 'To secure for the workers by hand or by brain the full fruits of their industry and the most equitable distribution thereof that may be possible on the basis of the common ownership of the means of production, distribution and exchange, and the best obtainable system of popular administration and control of each industry or service.' Common ownership must be for the benefit of all citizens.

An amendment must take into account the type of economy that is preferred; a 'free economy' is analogous to a jungle as the 'survival of the fittest' implies, but a 'controlled economy' is analogous to a prison. The concept of democracy implicates the concepts of freedom and equality, so a 'mixed economy' is the rational choice. The paragraph should have been amended as follows: 'To strive for the equitable distribution of wealth amongst all citizens; also, to secure the common ownership of seven basic utilities, that is, British Gas, British Railways, British Telecom, the Coal Industry, the Post Office, the Power & Electricity Network and the Water Companies which henceforth shall be known as the Magnificent Seven Utilities.' Ownership, whether private or public is not the deciding factor in the economic environment. Private ownership is severely limited in decision-making policy as the end is profit, whereas public ownership is non-profit making and can choose different ends in serving the public interest.

In 1964, the Labour Government inherited a critical 'balance of payments' problem which required some bitter medicine to be swallowed to cure the *disequilibrium.* It was too bitter and a Conservative Government was elected in 1970. By 1974, the 'balance of payments' had deteriorated again and a Labour Government was elected to solve the problem. Since 1945, the 'balance of payments' has been the *Achilles heel* in the UK economy. Any deficit in the current account is cancelled out by borrowing from the capital account. In 1979, the markets showed more confidence in sterling as North Sea oil began to flow more rapidly, and it was assumed by many economists that the UK 'balance of payments' would be favourable for a long time. Simultaneously, it was assumed that a Conservative Government was more competent to manage the economy. The question that was never asked—how long is a long period? The exports of oil peaked in 1985 and the next year, the 'balance of payments' was unfavourable once again.

Balance of Payments: Current Account

£ billion

	1987	1988	1989	1990	1991	1992	1993
Credits							
Exports	79.1	80.3	92.1	101.7	103.4	107.3	121.4
Invisibles	79.2	87.3	107.2	114.5	114.6	108.4	116.7
Total	158.3	167.6	199.3	216.2	218.0	215.7	238.1
Debits							
Imports	90.7	101.8	116 .8	120.5	113.7	120.4	134.8
Invisibles	72.4	82.3	104.9	115.0	112.8	104.8	114.3
Total	163.1	184.1	221.7	235.5	226.5	225.2	249.1
Balance							
	-4.8	-16.5	-22.4	-19.3	-8.5	-9.5	-11.0
Balance of Payments: Oil Analysis							
Exports	8.4	6.0	5.9	7.5	6.7	6.6	7.9
Imports	4.2	3.2	4.6	6.0	5.5	5.1	5.5
Balance	4.2	2.8	1.3	1.5	1.2	1.5	2.4

When reflecting upon the proceeds from the sales of the national assets and the total contribution of over £100 billion from North Sea oil, then no other conclusion can be drawn than that the UK has managed its house extremely inefficiently. After North Sea oil production had peaked, some politicians boasted about the economic miracle, but it was really an economic mirage. Focussing on the income/expenditure and balance of payments deficits, how much longer can the double deficits continue before drastic action is considered implicating a period of austerity. Temperance must replace extravagance.

Emile Durkheim taught that laws governing society could not be derived from biology or psychology; they 'exist outside the individual consciousness.' The significant contrast between economics and sociology is that economics must involve individualism whereas sociology does not. Economists insist that competition is necessary for economic progress. The question arises—is extreme competition innate and a part of human nature? The economic system demands that some must suffer misery for others to survive. Empiricism informs us that too much competition acts **like a** drug, it produces psychological side-effects in the form of fear and anxiety. Fear of failure in the classroom, on the farm, in the factory, running a business can lead to tragedy. It is inevitable that fierce competition when the stakes are high leads to cheating and dishonesty. The win at any cost behaviour affects the moral fabric of society in which self-interest and greed pervade.

In recent years, severe competition and the pursuit of profit has had an impact upon job security. The fear of redundancy and the loss of status causes anxiety which affects a person's health. The greatest distress of the long-term unemployed is related to loss of status; they feel that they are no longer normal members of society as they have no means of earning a living. A basic human need is disciplined work, not just solely for income, but it allows human beings to use their energies and develop their faculties. Throughout the world, technology has changed the structure of industry from labour intensive to capital intensive, and in the economic system, robots are now considered more valuable than human beings.

Chapter 8
Education and Etiquette

In recent times, education policy has been kicked about like a political football, yet education is society's most valuable resource. Since the Cartesian Revolution, man has attempted to conquer Nature and make her his slave, but he ignored the fact that human nature is a part of Nature. It is not Nature directly that supplies our most valuable resource, it is man or more precisely the mind of man. A mind that has been trained to seek knowledge, discover and invent. However, first, all minds have to be developed by a lengthy process of instruction to understand both visible and invisible things; the latter are just as significant as the former.

The evidence abounds to confirm that society is in a miserable state, which points to the fact that its education system for children and adults is inefficient. Most parents desire their children to obtain the best education possible. It has been repeated many times by politicians and others that children must be trained to participate in the world of technology. This scientific and technological world involves a special type of education which requires a set of techniques for imparting knowledge and skills. Accordingly, English, mathematics and science are the core subjects, the pursuit of wisdom is treated as an idle pastime, yet the state of existing society cries out for wisdom. The call for more resources to be ploughed into education is futile unless the harvest is more wisdom. Of course, wisdom entails values, and scientists have persistently claimed that science must be value-free. This is the social paradox; any rational education system must include a set of values which raises the question—what in our education system is thought to be valuable as an end?

Without any doubt, there is a crisis in our education system, and it is not the fault of the teaching profession, it is the fault of society. Many teachers have a difficult task in achieving their goals. Is it possible to teach children who exhibit aggressive behaviour, who use foul and abusive language, and who sometimes assault their teacher? Is it possible to teach children who are not mentally alert through lack of sleep due to late night TV viewing, or to teach children whose parents have neglected their duty to instil discipline. In the pursuit of knowledge, persistence and discipline are indispensable factors.

Besides the national curriculum, many teachers have become involved in drug and sex education. Also, many teachers are now acting the role of social worker, parent, therapist, security officer, health inspector and statistician. Why have teachers been loaded with these extra burdens? The cause can be traced to family breakdown, whereby divorce compels children to live with either their mother or father. Unfortunately, the rate of increase in divorce is an indication of a frequent breakdown in human relationships, and the child suffers in an environment which lacks love.

Human relationships are built upon the respect for another person from which trust emerges and love develops. Some psychologists have warned that if our technological society fails to understand our biological needs for love and companionship, the alternative is a society full of hate, of families engaged in bitter conflict, of teenagers seeking escape via alcohol or drugs, and children imitating the violent actions shown on TV. This is part of the social problem; society has so much faith in science, yet science steers clear of the emotions or the spiritual part of a human being. Therefore, science has limited usefulness; just as theology in the past was a deception, so today science involves fraud.

Religion provides human beings with guidance and the meaning of 'being' that science can never provide, and true religion relates to ethics. Of course, religion implicates the existence of a supreme being, and for many persons, this is unacceptable. The atheist is just as dogmatic as he presumes that man is the highest level of being. **Plato** possessed a gifted ability to recognise a problem which is a pre-requisite for solving a problem. To those who doubt that Plato can be accepted as an authority on education, then it is pertinent to recall some of the educational reforms that he recommended. His chief conviction was that education must be compulsory for every child in the State. Such a radical idea was not introduced into this country until 1876. Further, in an age of male dominated societies, he advocated that females should receive the same education as males. In the *Laws,* he advised that pregnant mothers must learn the importance of gentleness and kindness during pregnancy and afterwards, for it is in infancy where impressions are deepest. Also, he insisted on the careful nursing of pregnant mothers to prevent them from any harmful pleasures or pains. In the first three years of infancy, the child was to be instructed in such a way that although loved, the child's will could not dominate. From the age of three to six, all the children were to be collected at the local 'sanctuary' in the care of nurses. Here is the concept of the modern nursery school.

Towards the beginning of the *Republic,* **Plato** thought that in any system of education there must be tranquillity of mind. Rear children in a beautiful environment; acquaint them with harmonious forms and melodious musical sounds, teach them gracious manners and refined intercourse, then their souls will develop harmony, grace and beauty; in other words, they will be taught a true sense of values. Conversely, rear children in a squalid environment consisting of high-density housing, high rise office blocks, drab car parks and barren motorways; acquaint them with ugly forms and discordant musical sounds, show them scenes depicting aggressive behaviour and foul dialogue, then their souls will develop ugliness, rudeness and aggressiveness, in other words, they will be taught a false sense of values. Children without values develop a philistine reaction to natural beauty, so they have an inclination to destroy the beauty they cannot recognise.

In his education system, **Confucius** insisted upon propriety and **Plato** required children to be taught gracious manners. Many of the younger generation jeer and sneer when criticised about their manners. A study revealed that children as young as five years of age are increasingly belligerent, have no respect for other children's property, have little respect for adults, and frequently use obscene language. Many children have no inclination to express gratitude or consideration; their vocabulary is devoid of expressions such as 'Thank you' or 'I am sorry.' St Paul exhorted: 'Always give thanks.' Good manners relate to the consideration of others and etiquette implicates rules of conduct. One of the finest rules of conduct originated from **Confucius**, 'Do not do to others what you would not like them to do to you.' Certainly, good manners ought to be practiced in the home, but today, the economic climate allows no time for such decency, remember, 'foul is useful.'

Although those with vested interests disagree, it is beyond argument that television has been a major cause in the deterioration of manners. A strange paradox has emerged; television teaches children how to behave, so is it any wonder that bad behaviour is the common trend? Programme makers are obsessed by depicting evil actions which influence young minds. In the twentieth century, many have been influenced by science and have accepted **Nietzche's** claim, 'God is dead,' so traditional values are no longer valid. The 50s was the age of lost empires; the 60s was the age of lost values, the permissive society emerged. The following decade saw the introduction of unashamed individualism or the social acceptance of self-expression and self-indulgence, and most motorists adopted the Me-first philosophy, so courtesy and respect for the highway code disappeared. The 70s was the 'silver age of selfishness;' the 80s was the age when the yuppie culture emerged and it is now referred to as the 'golden age of greed.' The 90s saw the beginning of the 'middle ages.'

Traditional wisdom gave this warning: 'There are troubled times ahead. For human beings will be lovers of themselves; they will only love money, and they will be boastful, proud, abusive, selfish, unforgiving, slanderous, devoid of self-control, full of hatred, violent, despisers of the good, treacherous, reckless, conceited, lovers of pleasure, preferably to lovers of God...ever learning, but never able to grasp the truth; children will be disobedient to parents, ungrateful and showing no piety.' (Paraphrased from 2 Timothy 3:1 to 7)

Plato referred to the balance sheet in human affairs by way of making this declaration: 'Children are the riches of men, the greatest of all their assets, and the entire future of their state depends on whether they turn out ill or well.' His education system involved more than the teaching of children merely to acquire facts; the teaching profession's main function is to strive to instil 'the virtue which is the master of all virtues—wisdom and reason and right attitude, with the passionate belief in their task.' They must aim to remove ignorance, and 'the greatest ignorance is when human beings do not love but hate what reason shows to be right.'

Again, referring to the *Republic,* **Plato** insisted, 'Games and physical training are essential for the building of the body and the maintenance of health, besides introducing a balance and correctness in the intellectual activities of the mind.' An athlete who shuns intellectual activity is a philistine possessing streaks of cruelty; a student who shuns physical training lacks strength of character and remains spiritless. A rational education system entails the insistence that the mind and the body pursue their activities in mutual spiritual harmony. Competition produces a desire to win, but such a desire must be controlled. **Newbolt** perceived the excesses that exist today: 'When the great *judge* (scorer, referee, umpire) comes to write against your name, He writes, not that you won or lost, but how you played the game.' Alas! In all sport today, the mere athlete is not only competitive but obsessed by winning because the 'rent of ability' is so high. Therefore, the temptation to cheat and foul is so dominant, whereupon sport is subject to the same widespread corruption that exists in commerce and politics.

The word 'GOOD' has caused confusion in its various uses as the following examples may demonstrate—a good person, a good thing, a good argument, a good robber, a good weapon, and a nuclear power station is a good investment. Problems arise when we use the word 'good' both as a noun and an adjective. However, it has been postulated that the highest good, *summon bonum,* is subject to two alternatives—(a) a thing or a distinctive characteristic alone has a greater degree of excellence than any other thing; (b) the complete situation consists of a greater good than any other. **Immanuel Kant** called (a) the *supremum bonum* and (b) the *summon bonum.* The two types of goodness are far different from the type of goodness that **Plato** had in mind. He was concerned with moral goodness relating to all human beings and their thoughts, intentions, desires and the establishment of their institutions.

Human behaviour in the field of science is only a part of the propensity to listen to the theme of truth: 'a close relationship with the eternal order of things and the music of the spheres.' All other human affairs are insignificant as **Plato** emphasised, 'the ignorance that harms human beings and society the most, is not the lack of knowledge in the world of science and technological affairs, but the lack of knowledge in spiritual affairs.' Therefore, the first priority in any educational system is not the teaching of technological details of mechanical and industrial arts, nor the teaching of scientific laws and methods, it is the teaching of the recognition and appreciation of values. When a person maintains the 'good' is indefinable, then intuition becomes the dictionary. When a person claims that absolute truth does not exist, then why should anyone accept that such an assertion is true? If a doctrine is no more true than an alternative doctrine, for example, creation and evolution, is it a logical possibility for both doctrines to be true?

In the current education system, children are taught the fundamental principles of mathematics and science, but they will be given no instruction about the limitations of such subjects. Mathematics and science can make no contribution to the problem of 'good' and 'evil,' or whether certain actions are 'right' or 'wrong.' Certainly, the mathematicians and scientists have a valid excuse; can any moral teacher make a significant contribution when television is so impressionable on children? In 'A Short Review of The Immorality and Profaneness of the English Stage,' **Jeremy Collier** wrote: 'the business of plays is to recommend virtue and to discountenance vice…to make Folly and Falsehood contemptible, and to bring everything that is ill under Infamy and Neglect.'

Teachers are aware of their nearly impossible task, so most children are left to determine their own behaviour and attempt to solve for themselves their own moral problems. This imposes a severe strain upon the child's mind, by compelling the child to make decisions which are beyond the ability of the child. To expect a child to make such decisions is absurd as the child has been denied the knowledge to make such decisions. Obviously, the child must make many mistakes which the libertarians claim is essential for free expression, yet the child has no chance of blaming an authority; he or she is responsible for his or her action. Is it any wonder that children form groups or gangs to spread social disorder and cause destruction to property? At an early stage, to give a child moral instruction and practical guidance is the art of living in a rational society; if the child is taught to sow good seed, then the child will be rewarded, but if the child sows bad seed, then the child will not be rewarded. It will save the child a great deal of trouble in finding out the difference between a right and wrong action.

Plato recognised that other subjects are important because of their contribution to the study of reality. One subject is that which instructs the child in accuracy, particularly the accuracy involved in counting, measuring and weighing. The child is taught to solve simple problems like, if you pay a greengrocer 96 pence for a dozen oranges, how much will you pay for four oranges? Now, the child believes that arithmetic is associated with greengrocers, so steps have to be taken to prove that there is no association. If pence is changed to x and oranges to y, whereby $96x=12y$, and then the child is asked what $4y$ equals, the child usually becomes confused. Arithmetic involves relations and not facts; it involves a relation between quantities and not between things. Arithmetic is indispensable to existing society, it is used to calculate, to forecast and in many cases to trick. Of course, in the latter case, we are entitled to ask— is cheating right or wrong? Can the child make such a judgement without instruction?

Besides the increase in knowledge and scientific discoveries since the era of **Plato**, a fundamental need has arisen in existing society; the need to earn a living for slavery is supposed to have been abolished. Another significant factor is that we now live in a machine age in which competition puts a premium upon time and speed. In so many instances, the machine has been considered more important than a human being. The human soul is slowly being starved through a lack of spiritual vitamins.

Society has rigidly followed the Cartesian Method; therefore, government's education policies are directed towards what is good for the economy rather than what is good for children and society. Politicians' images have been tarnished because of their continuous attachment to double standards. Without doubt, our standard of living has improved, but primarily due to working wives supplementing the family income. Alas! A price has to be paid, and children have suffered in the transaction. The chief inspector of schools reported that the standards of numeracy and literacy in many cases is appalling.

So, often when the child returns home from school, there is no guiding hand to direct the child to beneficial habit-forming, so the need for discipline remains unsatisfied which is the indispensable requirement for study. It has been exaggerated that self-education is the only education; this is only partly true, nevertheless, it highlights the fact that the learning process does not cease in the classroom, it continues or ought to continue in the home.

In an important work 'The Psychology of Man's Possible Evolution,' **PD Ouspensky** noted that a person's attention can be in three distinctive parts—the mechanical part, the emotional part and the intellectual part. He wrote, 'With attention non-existent, or with attention wandering, we are in the mechanical part; with the attention attracted by the subject of observation or reflection and kept there, we are in the emotional part; with the attention controlled and held on the subject by will, we are in the intellectual part.' Mind wandering is often a condition of a child, so attention is lacking.

One of the foundation subjects in the national curriculum is music and this most popular art played an important part in **Plato's** education system. In the *Laws,* the Athenian Stranger continued his discussion: 'I began this discussion by saying that all children being naturally excitable by nature cannot remain quiet in either body or voice, but are constantly shouting and jumping about in a disorderly way. Then I went on to point out that only mature adults achieve a sense of order in these two distinctive parts. Orderly movement is called rhythm and the orderly expression in low and high tones is called harmony, while the two together form choral dance and song.'

Plato thought that any change in the type of music must be a cause for inquiry, 'Good education and upbringing, if preserved, will lead to human beings of a better nature, and these in turn, if they cling to their education will improve with each generation.' How can music be defined? Music is sound that we pick up as sound waves at different frequencies. **Pythagoras** pulled tight a string between two fixed points; he plucked at the string heavily and lightly only to discover the pitch of the note remained the same. To produce a higher note, he either had to increase the tension in the string or use a thinner string. The string in tension may vibrate 256 cycles per second which is equivalent to a note in tune with 'middle C' on a piano. If the string is divided into two loops, the vibration will be twice as fast, equivalent to 512 cycles per second which is in tune with the note an octave (eight notes) higher. In the scale of **C,** the root chord is **(C E G)** and **Pythagoras** found simple mathematical relationships exist. The note **E** vibrates at a ratio of 5:4 with 'middle **C;**' **E** vibrates five times as middle **C** vibrates four times; the note **G** vibrates at a ratio of 3:2 with 'middle **C;**' **G** vibrates three times as middle **C** vibrates twice.

A scale is a series of eight sounds produced in alphabetical sequence from a selected note to its octave. The sounds conform to a set arrangement of tones and semitones. There are two types of scales—*chromatic* and *diatonic; the chromatic* scale is composed of only 12 semitones whereas the *diatonic* scale is composed of two semitones and five tones. It is best to consider the 12 semitones as 12 half steps, a half step being the shortest distance between two keys when following a horizontal line across the black and white keys.

In the illustration, we can see that a black key is positioned between two white keys which is a half-step away from either white key. For example, the black key positioned between the white keys **C-D** is equivalent to **C** sharp or **D** flat. Similarly, the black key between **F-G** is equivalent to **F** sharp or **G** flat. The white keys are called Naturals and the black keys are called Sharps or Flats. A Sharp allows a note to be raised one semitone or a half step higher; a Flat allows a note to be reduced one semitone or a half step lower. Notice that no black key is placed between the white keys **E-F and B-C.**

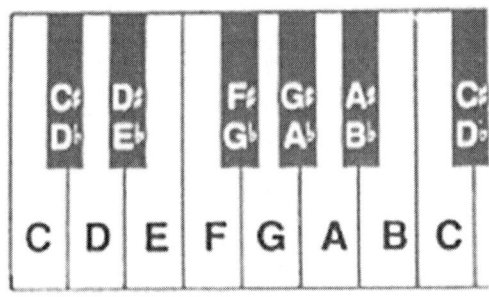

As there is no black key between **E-F** and **B-C,** there is a semitone or a half step between both **E-F** and **B-C,** so that the key **E** is also **F** flat and the key **F** is also **E** sharp. Similarly, the key **B** is also **C** flat and the key **C** is also **B** sharp. In any scale, there are special note names, so let us consider the note names in the scale of **C** Major.

1st Note **C=Tonic**	2nd Note **D=Supertonic**
3rd Note **E=Mediant**	4th Note **F=Sub-dominant**
4th Note **G=Dominant**	6th Note **A=Sub-mediant**
7th Note **B=Leading Note**	8th Note **C=Upper Tonic**

Let us consider the octave comprising the eight notes in the **C major scale;** the tones and semitones are arranged in two equal parts. Each part is called a *tetrachord* meaning a scale of four notes; the two *tetrachords* form the complete scale via the insertion of a tone between them as shown below.

Scale of C Major

```
                        Tone
C Tone D Tone E Semi-F ---------G Tone A Tone B Semi-C
          Tone                            Tone
```
Lower Tetrachord   **Upper Tetrachord**

The Tonic is the key note and denotes the name of the scale. The Dominant is five notes above the Tonic and it has a significant influence in determining the key. The formation of the sharp scales is derived from the two *tetrachords* in the scale of **C.** The scales must conform to the *diatonic* pattern and the second tetrachord starting with the dominant note **G** is used for the first tetrachord of a different scale. The exercise is repeated throughout until the key with seven sharps is reached. The formation of flat scales is a similar operation and they are also derived from the two *tetrachords* in the scale of **C**.

The flat scales must conform to the *diatonic* pattern and the second *tetrachord* starting with the sub-dominant note **F** is used for the first *tetrachord* of a different scale. The exercise is repeated throughout until the key with seven flats is reached. Minor scales conform to a different *diatonic* pattern as the tones and semitones are arranged differently. Two forms of the minor scale exist—the Harmonic and the Melodic.

Musical sounds are represented by symbols placed on or between parallel lines called a *stave.* At first, the *stave* was formed by eleven parallel lines equally spaced which was called the *Great Stave.* The notes were not easy to read, so the *Great Stave* was divided into two equal sections, a top *stave* and a bottom *stave* each having five parallel lines. A short line below the top *stave* or above the bottom *stave* may be drawn to accommodate middle **C** which allows note **B** to be placed under the line and **D** above the line. The top *stave* is known as the treble or **G** clef and the bottom *stave* the bass or **F** clef; the two *staves* are usually joined by a bracket.

The Treble Clef **G** ls set on the 2nd line

The Bass Clef F is set on the 4th line

Music includes **melody,** which is an agreeable sequence of single tones; **rhythm** which involves the movement of sound relating to time and speed; **harmony** which involves chords, a combination of notes sounded together. The duration of notes are subject to some form of time clock, which nearly all human beings possess relating to their sense of rhythm. The measure of notes implicates a whole note and its fractions. The table **explains.**

a whole note=a **Semibreve**	generally 4 beats
a 1/2 note=a **Minim**	2 beats
al 1/4 note=a **Crotchet**	1 beat
a 1/8 note= a **Quaver**	1/2 beat
a 1/16 note=a **Semiquaver**	1/4 beat
a 1/32 note=a **Demisemiquaver**	1/8 beat

Sometimes, a note needs to be prolonged by half of its duration, so a dot is placed after the note; in the case of the minim, this is equal to three beats; in the case of a crotchet, this is equal to one and half beats. Short vertical lines, called Bar Lines are drawn across the staves at certain intervals and between two bar lines it is known as a Bar or a Measure. Time is shown by two figures at the beginning of a musical composition and is called the Time-Signature; it is positioned directly after the key-signature. On occasions, the duration of one note in a bar needs to be extended to the next bar which is accomplished by a tie or a short curve. In rhythm notation, it may appear paradoxical, but silence needs to be measured as well as sound. Silence involves rest from sound, so for every note value there is a corresponding *rest.*

Harmony involves chords and a chord is two or more notes played simultaneously. A triad is a chord composed of three notes; the tone upon which a chord is constructed is called the 'Root.' The identity of a chord root always appears first, such as 'C maj,' or 'F maj 7.' Suppose we wish to construct a major chord with C as the root, so starting with the note C, we move 4 half steps higher to arrive at the second tone of the chord which is E; moving another 3 half steps higher then we arrive at the third tone of the chord which is G. All major triads can be obtained by the formula, Root-4 half steps-3 half steps. There are formulae for all other types of chords. Of course, chords may also be used in their inversions. Consider the CEG chord; the first inversion is EGC and the second inversion is GCE. Our experience of harmony instructs us that only certain chords can be used in any set key. Again, using our key-signature of C whose major chord is CEG, we can use the major chord of F which is FAC; C is a common tone to both chords. Also, we can use the major chord of G which is GBD; G is a common tone.

Like physics, music has its own vocabulary, especially for the tone and the speed. The expression of a musical composition is indicated by certain Italian words such as *Pianissimo* or *Fortissimo* meaning very soft and very loud. **Shakespeare** wrote, 'The man that hath no music in himself, nor is not moved by concord of sweet sounds, Is fit for treasons, strata-gems and spoils....Let no such man be trusted.'

The dualism in man's nature has been acknowledged for over two thousand years, one part brute, the other part human, and this realisation has motivated some men to strive to become super-human so the brutish part is eliminated. **Tennyson,** at the end of *In Memoriam* makes this appeal:

...Arise and fly
The reeling Faun, the sensual feast;
Move upward, working out the beast,
And let the ape and tiger die.

Such an appeal today falls on deaf ears. The Establishment by its proneness to maintain the *status quo* together with its economic determinism refuses to face the reality screaming out; **Rousseau's** 'noble savage' has emerged; however, freed from any ethical values, behaviour reduces to that of the brutes; thus the deeds are anything but noble. Those who deny there exists a social problem need to remove their rose-tinted glasses. Children ought to be made aware of the distinction between a brute and a human being. At an appropriate time, their attention should be drawn to **St Paul's** letter to the Philippians which contains one of the fundamental beliefs on which our culture has developed, paraphrased below: '...whatsoever things are true, whatsoever things are noble, whatsoever things are just, whatsoever things are beautiful, whatsoever things are of good account; if anything relates to virtue and warrants praise, think about these things.'

This part of the letter was the core of neo-classical thought until the 'theory of evolution' was thrust upon a gullible society. Despite the disagreement among scientists about **Darwin's** Theory, it is suggested that the theory has been accepted as an established fact by our educational authorities. Yet a physicist, **Paul Davies** wrote: 'If the universe is simply an accident, the odds against it containing any amount of order is ludicrously small. If the BIG BANG was just a random event, then as near as probability is to certainty the emergent cosmic material world would have been in thermodynamic equilibrium at maximum entropy. As this was certainly not the case, the conclusion must be that the actual state of the universe has been CHOSEN from a huge number of alternative states.' Temptation cannot be resisted; who chose our existing state?

In his excellent book, *God: To be or not to be?* which is mainly a critical analysis of Monad's scientific materialism, **A Ernest Wilder-Smith** refuted the theory of evolution. He maintained that natural selection is extremely wasteful of material compared to conceptual thought selection in the production of biological variety. He was convinced that the codes of life could never have emerged from the randomness of matter: 'We are driven thus to accept the stimulatory code mechanism which is one of **thought** as the source of information and its storage behind the genetic code and not the try and see method.' Where did the information originate to form the genetic code? Dr Wilder-Smith concluded, 'Thus the Darwinian argument inevitably brings us to the point where we deny that God is the *logos,* for *logos* is thought and not its opposite, namely, chance or non-thought. The choice is the *logos* or randomness.' He emphasised that to reject the *logos* in favour of chance is, in the final analysis to reject the second law of thermodynamics; likewise, to assert the mind is full of randomness is to deny the activity of mind.

Two eminent scientists have submitted a powerful refutation of evolutionism on purely rational grounds which leads to the conclusion that Darwin's Theory equates to science fiction. When science intrudes into the field of faith, then it forfeits its principle of verification; moreover, our fundamental convictions are derived from philosophy and not from science. Once upon a time, children were taught about 'Natural Law,' and that the 'Laws of Nature' implicate a higher level of being. The **Duke of Wellington** foresaw the consequences of excluding religious study from the national curriculum, 'Educate children without religion, and you make them but clever devils.'

Chapter 9
Homes and Health

It is impossible to confine this treatise to the chapter title, as it cannot be separated from 'Environment and Energy' and 'Transport and Travel.' The former is associated with the location, design and space of a home, the latter to the resident's place of work, schools and shops and the means of getting to them. In an unpredictable climate, people need shelter or a house for just the same reason as they need food, water and clothing, namely, for keeping the body in a condition of homeostasis or physiological equilibrium. Economic theory makes no distinction between a house and a home. A house is a physical structure whereas a home is regarded as a social, economic and cultural institution. To assert that a home is a good investment is typical of our materialistic society. The Bible reveals a far different concept; a home is a place of rest and meditation as well as other activities in the home. It is written, 'My people shall live in peaceful dwellings.'

A housing problem has existed throughout our social history but the magnitude of our problem has developed from the Victorian Era. During this era, after our industrial revolution had commenced, family planning was almost non-existent. The stock of housing had to be expanded in an attempt to keep pace with the expanding population. Of course, two significant considerations occur in any housing analysis—one is the quantity of houses and the other is the quality. In the rush to partially satisfy the demand for houses, the quality factor was disregarded, so that living conditions affected the health of the occupants. As John Bull's industrial locomotive developed, full steam towns began to grow around the factories. Large contract building became the fashion where the profit motive prompted the skimping of materials and shoddy workmanship. Jerry building became the name of the game and even with all the building regulations, the game continues. The word was derived from the shipping terms 'jerry-rig' or 'jerry-mast' which were temporary poles of low-grade timber. External walls were only four and half inch single course and such a thickness is not adequate to resist high wind loadings, consequently the nine-inch English bond wall became standard practice. Living in a through-terrace house was the highest step on the property ladder for a few exceptionally skilled workers. It was referred to as two up and two down with a yard at the rear where access was available from an alley and the only luxury was a WC at the bottom of the yard. Such squalid conditions were reflected in the Act of Parliament—the Housing of the Working Classes Act of 1890.

The following is a portion of the King's speech delivered to the representatives of the local authorities and societies at Buckingham Palace in 1919.

> While the housing of the working classes has always been a question of the greatest social importance, never has it been so important as now. It is not too much to say that an adequate solution of the housing question is the foundation of all social progress...The first point that the attack must be delivered is the unhealthy, ugly, overcrowded houses in the mean street, which all us know too well. If a healthy race is to be reared, it can be reared only in healthy homes; if drink and crime are to be successfully combated, decent, sanitary houses must be provided; if 'unrest' is to be converted into contentment...

The standard of working-class houses improved considerably after the King's speech due to the development of council estates by local authorities. However, the housing problem showed no signs of solution as private builders declined to build for landlords and those that **were** built for letting, the rent demanded was too high for low wage-earners. Up until the Second World War, the average working man was paying a third of his wages to the landlord. In 1995, the average working man was paying half of his wages to either a landlord or a building society. Before 1990, negative equity had never been a problem although a 15% mortgage interest rate was not new.

Between the two wars, a slight increase in home ownership or rather home mortgages became the trend, although the burden was mainly limited to white collar workers and higher wage-earning skilled workers. The increased desire to purchase a three-bedroom semi-detached house or two-bedroom bungalow had been urged by the economic state that caused the reduction in material and wage costs. The building societies average interest rate was four and a half per cent which was consistent with the usury laws in the previous century prohibiting interest rates of more than five per cent. Usury was conceived as a form of theft, but the worshipping of the free market changed the conception. In the nineteen thirties, a three-bedroom semi-detached house in a suburban area cost approximately £650, and after a 10% deposit had been paid, the monthly repayment amounted to approximately £4.50.

In the early twenties, the concept of the 11-inch cavity wall was incorporated in superior properties in place of the 9-inch solid brick wall. The cavity wall consisted of an exterior course of stock bricks and an internal course of soft flettons. The concept of the cavity wall was based on the belief that driving penetrating rain could not penetrate the inner course because of the 2-inch air gap. Unfortunately, little attention was paid to the corrosive property of the steel ties that tied the two courses of bricks. However, jerry-builders refused to build 11-inch cavity wall properties, but preferred the cost cutting method of building 9-inch solid brick walls with soft flettons and then rendering or stone-dashing the exterior face. The thermal resistance of the walls was poor and as most properties had a chimney breast in every room, the environment was cold and damp. Another factor that accounted for a considerable amount of heat loss was the installation of galvanised steel window frames which were not only draughty but produced severe condensation problems.

The internal design of properties was the subject of two viewpoints, the architects and the builders. The significant difference was whether living space should be designed to partition rooms for a particular use or one room serving multiple purposes. Usually, pre-war houses were designed with three rooms on the ground floor; a front or sitting room, a small dining room adjoining a small kitchen. Post-war, most builders, to save the cost of building a single course partition wall, combined the sitting room and the dining room. However, the majority thought that a separate dining room was preferable as it allowed the children to be isolated so that they might play on the dining room table or do their homework.

Post-war housing was influenced by the introduction of various household appliances on the market which dictated the requirement of larger kitchens and more electrical socket outlets; in other words, the demand for energy in the home was rapidly increasing. The old system of electrical wiring installation used a 2-

core rubber or lead sheathed cable wired to either a 5-amp or 15-amp power point. This has been superseded by the ring main system with double conductors fused at 30 amp at the main fuse board, and then forming a ring circuit, looping in and out of 13-amp socket outlets with their appliance plugs separately fused. The introduction of PVC sheathed cables though not as flexible as rubber sheathed cables offset this by having greater current carrying capacity. Unfortunately, in any business enterprise, profit is the chief consideration and so long as the work is done, that is all that matters. How the job is done is hardly considered, consequently, the layout of the wiring in most homes is chaotic. In the lighting circuit, some contractors looped out from a ceiling rose, others from a switch and some used a junction box for looping out the live wire; cable runs and layouts were seldom planned; today, most loop out from a ceiling rose.

Another development in post-war housing was the demand for a central heating system. The previous method of heating a room was via a coal fire, but by installing a boiler at the rear of the fire, it enabled domestic water to be heated in a galvanised steel tank. An independent solid fuel boiler situated in the kitchen had a higher heat output, so besides heating the domestic water, it was possible to heat two or three radiators. A big disadvantage of the system was the circulation of the water was natural, therefore, it required the use of 1.25-inch pipes which were an eyesore. Coal fires contributed to the smog in the early fifties which prompted the government to pass 'The Clean Air Act' of 1956 which was instrumental in reducing smoke and smog in towns. The discovery of North Sea gas began to challenge 'King Coal' and the proposal for forced water circulation confined the boiler to the kitchen.

A factor unmentioned up to this point relates to the housing problem; it is the first factor of production, namely, land. Prices of land have varied throughout the country since the early nineteenth century, although it is possible to report an average price in a certain area at a certain time. In the thirties, a plot of development land could be purchased in a London suburb for £5 per foot, but land a little more rural was bought for £100 an acre, so depending upon the density of the housing, a plot could be bought much cheaper. Post-war land prices more than doubled with a corresponding increase in the price per acre. As the demand for building land became insatiable, the large building contractors insisted on designs to suit the narrowest plots. In housing design, few have had real freedom of choice; the developer decides on the design and the property is built; it is advertised for sale and the attitude is, take it or leave it.

The greater demand for land can be verified by the change in direction that occurred in the fifties and sixties; instead of building out, it was decided to build up; tenements in the sky were thought to be the celestial answer to the housing problem. High-rise flats answered the demand for higher densities in the cities, (approx. 1SO persons per acre) although flats of a smaller storey height were built elsewhere. As we know, the high-rise flat experiment has proved an extremely expensive failure, both financially and psychologically. The crying shame is that the waste of resources could have been avoided if a meta-physical judgement had been made, but bigotry prevailed. Ecology was in its infancy and anyone who suggested that man must live in accordance with nature was labelled eccentric. In 1968, the Ronan Point disaster made the architectural profession acutely aware of the misconceived notion that was advocating the construction of high-rise flats.

In the design of properties, another important factor is the roof design, or more precisely, the nature of the framework of the roof. There has been a tendency in post-war roof design to opt for a shallow roof pitch varying from 22 to 25 degrees. In high winds, this can lead to tiles being dislodged and blown from roofs which was a frequent occurrence during the mini-hurricane in 1987. The term pitch was interpreted as either the ratio of the roof to its span, or the number of degrees in the angle which the roof makes to the horizontal. Obviously, the correct pitch for a roof is determined to a large extent by the nature of the covering. It needs no explanation to perceive that the steeper the roof pitch, the more quickly rain and snow are dispelled and the less likely will there be any water penetration by driving rain between the tiles. Whether the tiles on a roof are subject to suction or compression by high wind loading is dependent upon the pitch of the roof. Before the advent of pre-fabricated trussed roof rafters using 25mm thick timber, most common rafters were 4inch by 2inch timber.

It has been recorded that there remained in Britain during 1971 a total of 1.76 million dwellings which have existed for more than one hundred years; in 1981, the total had increased to 2.4 million and by 2008 it increased to 4.6 million. Further, the number of unfit dwellings now amounts to over 8 million. Such figures show the magnitude of the problem, especially when politicians boast about the increase in property ownership when there is an appalling neglect of property maintenance. The constant propaganda associated with a property-owning democracy in the past, gives the impression that owning property for owning's sake is a good thing, whereas owning a minute portion of the earth's assets entails responsibility. What is required is a change of attitude for the housing problem is much greater than most people think. It is inevitable that as the owners of property reach the age of retirement then their amount of energy is reduced, so they are unable to undertake the amount of maintenance which was previously done. If the owners cannot afford to pay someone else to maintain their property, then neglect and deterioration is the result.

Dependent upon fate, a man may play three roles at different times in society—he may study to become an *engineer;* then, by acquiring financial knowledge, he may be persuaded to become a *managineer;* then, quite possibly after frustration and disillusionment, he may be motivated to become an *imagineer.* Imagineering is not a science but more of an art; it may be defined as thinking about the future consequences of human actions and imagining beneficial changes for society; it is a value dominated preoccupation. The *imagineer* proceeds from this axiom; meticulous planning and effective control are essential in any rational society. Such a society depends not solely upon scientific and economic judgements but on metaphysical and ethical judgements as well.

It is obvious indeed, that no change of system or machinery can avert those causes of social *malaise* which consist in the egotism greed, or quarrelsomeness of human nature. What it can do is to create an environment in which this behaviour is not encouraged. It cannot compel men to live in accordance with certain principles. What it can do is to establish a social system upon set principles which, if they are influenced, they can live in accordance to these principles.

The perception of **RH Tawney** is just as significant today as it was nearly a century ago except that the *malaise* has extended to our socio-cultural and bio-physical environment. It has often been claimed that we are a wealth-creation society and we have become victims of our own success. What a distortion of logic! The fact is that we have wasted a colossal amount of resources, suggests that we have become victims of our own stupidity and this undesirable habit shows no sign of being broken.

The poor performance in managing our house will inevitably lead to an aggravation of the housing problem. **Goethe** made **Faust** say, 'Men jeer at what they do not understand.' Here is a fact which strangles any inclination to jeer;

the resources of the earth are finite; therefore, economic growth is a limited option. To maintain or increase sales, industrial corporations have employed two artifices, namely, planned obsolescence and built-in deterioration which certainly precipitates waste. It becomes manifest that houses in the future will have to be built to a design and specification far different to existing designs and specifications. There is widespread interest in low-energy house development but this tackles only a part of the problem. In the long term, it is irrational to design any house encompassing a high thermal resistance if the exterior walls have been built with facing bricks. It is hoped that no false impression has been made about energy efficiency, but it cannot be too strongly emphasised that the amount of heat required to maintain an optimum temperature in a building is related to the volume of air to be heated. This is why churches, cathedrals, castles, palaces and mansions have such a cold feeling because with any heat input, hot air rises and the heat losses in such buildings are high. Heat from mainly radiation was the only answer in the past which meant that persons had to be in close proximity to the heat source. Large offices, factories, warehouses and supermarkets would be unbearably cold if there was not an adequate heat input.

Although energy efficiency is important, in future, the design of the dwelling will be the first consideration. House designs of 1,000 square feet or more will no longer be an option, thus the area of living space must be carefully studied in future housing designs. The family unit of husband, wife and three or more children is no longer the average. Many households today consist of single persons or single-parent families. Many middle-aged couples move to a bungalow after their children have left their home. Also, a greater number of households are occupied by elderly persons. The conclusion to be drawn is that the greatest demand is for either single- or two-bedroom properties. Now, it is common knowledge that a flight of stairs and landing take up a considerable amount of space in any house, but the main advantage in house design is that it demands less frontage than a bungalow.

The reluctance of builders to build bungalows is because the design demands a frontage of at least 10 metres and they also have a large roof area. However, the 'bangla' of Bengal or bungalow appears to be the home which is most needed and it is far easier to maintain than a house. The first thing to be considered is the pitch of the roof and it is recommended that a height to span ratio of 9:20 be considered. Obviously, the wider the span of the roof trusses, then the higher the ridge and the greater area of roof covering. From an imagineering aspect, the spans of bungalows implicating the internal dimension between the two opposite external walls supporting the roof trusses ought to be 5 to 6 metres. With such a span and the recommended roof pitch, the ridge is not in the stratosphere and the area of roof covering is not excessive. The most suitable type of roof is the hipped type, no gable ends with overhanging eves. Well-burned stock bricks are desirable for external walls with cellular blocks for internal walls, and 50mm studs fastened to them and fibreglass slabs inserted between them. All internal partition walls should be constructed via timber studs.

The amount of living space required is a controversial subject but those who prefer small dance halls instead of one-metre-wide passageways is no longer an option. Also, it displays a false sense of values when opting to have a garage situated under the same roof as the inhabitants. It appears that it is necessary to consider the homeostatic condition of a physical object just like a human being. Including a garage within cavity walls and a tiled roof framework is a sheer waste of resources. Of course, a motor vehicle requires space, not only when in motion but also when at rest, and undoubtedly, the use of the motor vehicle has caused a major environmental problem. Reverting to the changes in society, there are many persons who have no time or interest in cultivating a garden, so a flat is the best type of property for such persons. However, for the single parent or a married couple with children, a garden is essential for not only teaching children about biology and ecology, but to encourage a respect for lower creation or *noblesse oblige.* They will soon come in contact with birds, bees, butterflies, ladybirds, spiders and worms. An apple tree ought to be planted in every garden, not only to keep the doctor away but to remind us of the truth in Genesis, namely, pride is a deadly sin. In 'God's Garden,' **Dorothy P Gurney** wrote:

> *The kiss of the sun for pardon,*
> *The song of the birds for mirth,*
> *One is nearer God's Heart in a garden*
> *Than anywhere else on earth*

Psychology leaves no doubt that a garden is a great asset to assist in the relieving of stress upon human beings, similar to the effect of normalising or stress relieving of steels, whereby a better grain structure is obtained. In the case of human beings, a better mind structure is obtained. In a society dominated by an economic determinism in which competition is the key to the mechanism, market forces dictate that financial costs shall be reduced to the minimum irrespective of the harm it causes to human beings. Therefore, our economic system is a major factor in imposing external pressures upon most human beings. In engineering science, stress is defined as 'force per unit area, but human stress is not so easy to define because psychological differences allow some human beings to cope better than others, especially in ruthless management decisions.' In the early part of his book on *pragmatism,* **William James** highlighted two main types of temperament—the tender-minded rationalist who is guided by principles, and the tough-minded empiricist who is guided by facts. In the business world, the latter is more useful than the former. However, human stress relates to the reaction to internal and external pressures; when the mind is unbalanced, then the body becomes unbalanced.

The state of equilibrium focuses attention on the biological needs to keep the human body in a state of physiological equilibrium or a homeostatic condition. The internal equilibrium of the body demands a stable chemical composition, blood temperature and oxygen supply. The fundamental biological needs are widely known-air, water, food, urination, excretion, lactation, sex, adequate rest and sleep. There is a need for shelter for the avoidance of abnormal temperature and discomfort from wind and rain. Also, there is a need for the avoidance of disagreeable stimuli as well as dangerous situations.

It has been well reported that fear is a serious risk factor to human well-being. Fear imposes a direct stress upon a person which is a direct cause of ill-health. **Hans Schafer** proclaimed at an international convention of physicians held at Davos in Switzerland, 'Health education must be carried on in harmony with moral demands' which is dependent upon 'reviving old religious values.' Undeniably, the acceptance of the theory of evolution and the rejection of religious doctrine has led to an increase in stress related diseases. Illness is not solely related to the disturbance in the chemical equilibrium of the body for there are other factors involved.

The chief factors are stress, nutrition deficiencies, air water and land pollution besides noise pollution; beside noise pollution; the upset of biological rhythms by an unnatural lifestyle lead to biological disorders. The effect of preventive medicine demands a healthy lifestyle.

The present and past government's policy on health care is to tackle the symptoms and not the cause. The King Lear attitude exists in all governments, so the attitude of the Pharisees reigns. By condemning the excessive consumption of alcohol as well as appealing for abstinence when driving a motor vehicle, then passing a law extending the licensing hours certainly leaves any government's judgement suspect.

The announcement by the Health Minister in March 1996 that there is the possibility of a link between BSE and CJD brought to the attention once again as to whether human beings should become vegans. Also, this ill-fated announcement allowed 'animal rights' activists to jump on the band-wagon. First, the desire that animals should have rights is absurd; rights are inextricably linked to respect; the lion, the tiger, the wolf, the crocodile or the shark have no respect for human beings, they are carnivores or flesh-eaters. It is doubtful whether any activist has been butted by a ram or chased by a bull. Further, rights entail responsibility and such an ethical concept does not exist in the animal kingdom. Primitive man was primarily a hunter and the bulk of his diet consisted of flesh. Now suddenly, primitive man acted unnaturally, he ought to have lived on leaves, berries and fruit. Man needs a balanced diet, so the balance is achieved by being part herbivore and part carnivore, in other words he is an omnivore. It was indicated that lactation is a basic human need especially for babies, so Daisy, our Friesian friend ought to be treated with more respect. It is a sad fact that Daisy is not treated as such, she is merely treated as a factor for production before she dries up after four or five years. Human beings have a relationship with animals and in any relationship there is right and wrong behaviour. To treat a domesticated animal as merely a factor of production is both cruel and merciless. Metaphysical errors are inevitable when animals are treated as machines and neglecting to understand the difference in 'being'. *Noblesse oblige* equates to a respect for lower creation.

Meat is the main source of high protein; the kind of protein which possesses the eight amino acids that the human body cannot produce. A deficiency in these amino acids causes protein deficiency in vegans. Another significant point; the vitamin B12 exists only in meat and animal products; it is indispensable in the production of blood. Vegans who do not have an adequate intake of the vitamin B12 are subject to the risk of anaemia. Even though vegans may have a similar intake of iron as omnivores, haemoglobin is less, due to the form in which the iron was absorbed, via meat or otherwise.

A few philosophers have argued that vegetarianism is the only ethically acceptable nourishment. They have insisted that an animal's interests be given equal consideration like a human being's interest. The case for animal rights emerges from the common conception of human rights, namely, human rights arc justified claims to the protection of a human being's most important interests.

In 'The Case for Animal Rights,' one academic philosopher argued that all animals are 'subjects of life' and for that reason alone, they have basic rights. By applying traditional logic, the two premises and conclusion can be obtained: 'Subjects of life' have basic rights;

Animals are 'subjects of life' therefore,

Animals have basic rights.

The second premise is true but controversy arises about the first premise. The second premise would remain true as follows:

Plants are 'subjects of life';

If we should eat animals flesh because they are 'subjects of life,' why should we eat plants?

Animals are only a part of the great chain of being in which they, minerals, plants and mankind have an inter-relationship with the living soil. The living soil is a priceless asset yet it is assumed to be the first factor of production. It is a metaphysical error to treat the living soil, plants and animals as having only utility. Their existence and inter-relationship with mankind reveals a plan and purpose; it is no mere 'chance'. The author willingly gives his support to 'Compassion in world Farming,' but he rejects the case for vegetarianism.

Chapter 10
Environment and Energy

No matter whether you are rich or poor, if you suffer from a serious disease, then your total assets or few possessions are of little account. After years of denying the reality, it is now recognised that society is suffering from a mental as well as an environmental malady. When the minds of human beings have been polluted by ideas claiming 'God is dead;' 'Morality depends upon the individual situation;' 'Absolute values are taboo;' is it any surprise that we are engaged in a war highlighting the futility of all wars? Can human beings win a war against nature? Environmental issues have become the fashion in politics. However, when a leading politician proclaimed, 'Economic delivery is the basis of all political power,' it is evident that politicians will treat environmental matters in just the same way as they have treated farming, housing, education, health and safety matters.

Via the media, we are conscious of the destruction of the environment through deforestation. Also, it is commonly known that forests are vital for the preservation of life on earth, and that almost fifty per cent of photosynthetic fixation of carbon from the atmosphere with its capacity to coincide with the release of oxygen is part of the nature of forests. Woodlands possess another important factor, namely, they control water supplies besides absorbing dust and noise. Tropical rain forests provide plants that are a key source of our food crops as well as supplying valuable medicines.

Deforestation causes three undesirable problems for human beings. The first problem has been well documented, the burning of huge quantities of trees causes carbon to be released into the atmosphere, thereby adding to the greenhouse gases. The other two problems relate to rain and drought. Without protection from the forest, rain erodes the soil, so that heavy rain causes floods, and with a reduction of moisture in the atmosphere, there is a tendency for droughts. The inescapable conclusion is that deforestation affects the global environment, so the problem is international rather than national. In major industrial nations, there is a reluctance to reduce energy consumption for such a policy would affect economic growth. This predicament shows that any real solution to the problem depends upon the realisation that economic growth exacerbates the problem.

Ecologists, **James Nations** and **Daniel Komer** believed that third world nations 'are merely pawns in a general's game. To understand the colonist's role in deforestation, one must ask why these families enter the rainforest in the first place. The answer is simple; for there is no land for them elsewhere.' Their choice is stark; either to die from malnutrition and starvation or to die from global pollution.

Although the destruction of the rainforests provide human beings with an environment of their own creation, so do the construction of cities. Cities produce air pollution; their high density population breathe air and exhale carbon dioxide; air is used to air-condition and heat their buildings; air is required in the fuel mixture of their motor engines, and by the incomplete combustion of hydrocarbon fuels, carbon monoxide is produced, which is toxic to both human beings and animals as well as plants. Noise is another form of city pollution, mainly from transportation systems although high powered amplifiers are another noise nuisance. City dwellers need a water supply plus a sewerage system and also a means of disposing of their waste. There are no holes in the ground of the city other than drains and an underground railway network.

Holes in the ground have been nearly all filled in some industrial nations, so they are now compelled to export their waste. Japan produces a huge amount of waste which it finds difficulty in exporting at a reasonable cost. Some western countries have similar problems and the demand for waste sites in third world countries is increasing, for much of the waste is toxic. The problem is developing to such an extent that many environmentalists claim that we are rapidly reaching the point when we will be buried in our own waste. It has been argued that there exist four methods of disposing of rubbish; bury the stuff, burn the stuff, recycle the stuff or produce less of the stuff. The first two answers create further problems, so that the latter two are the best solutions.

Burying all kinds of rubbish can create health problems to residents who live in close proximity to the site. As the waste products decompose beneath the surface of the earth, an odourless inflammable gas is caused by the decomposition. Methane gas may drift underground outside the bounds of the site destroying plant life and leak into the homes of human beings with the possibility of causing an explosion. Explosion is the appropriate word to associate with chemical wastes dumped in holes in the ground for in reality such dumps are minefields. The significant question needs to be answered—how many minefields are there in Great Britain? After the chemical horror which occurred at Seveso, a horrified Italian observer wrote, 'Our unconditional faith in science and its ability to cure the world of its ills is ended.'

The wastes that have been examined are one of two kinds—bio-degradable or toxic. However, there is a far more lethal form, nuclear waste. At the beginning of the fifties an argument abounded, relating to the question, 'Ought man to split atoms?' The argument oscillated between two main groups; a tender-minded group who argued from the authority of metaphysics, and a tough-minded group who argued from the authority of economics. History records who won the argument but it will also record the tragic mistake made by human beings. All those in favour of continuing to split atoms in nuclear power plants were strongly influenced by economic expediency rather than by metaphysical judgement. The irrationality that prevailed at that time can be appreciated by the fact, that those who claimed that harnessing nuclear energy was both unsafe for the existing generation and future generations were compelled to prove their case. On the other hand, those who were in favour of the so-called peaceful use of nuclear energy were not compelled to prove that its use was safe or that there would be any future harmful consequences for human beings. This gross distortion of logic, allied to a false value judgement, prompted many intellectuals to distrust the judgement of politicians which pointed to a serious defect in the democratic system.

Of course, all but few jumped on the nuclear roller-coaster because it was a new source of energy which would be required to replace fossil fuels in the future and it was asserted that it would be low in price. The assertion has proved to be false, yet it was so predictable when the capital cost calculations were forecast on a 6% interest rate, plus a 2% surplus capital allowance. As nuclear power entails a capital-intensive technology compared with most conventional alternatives, the interest rate employed in the calculation of capital charges and the accumulation of depreciation allowances was of central importance. In the cost-benefit analysis of nuclear power, the benefits were reduced to a price, but the price that was disregarded was the one that future generations will have to pay.

In a report on the 'Control of Pollution,' submitted in February 1972 to the Secretary of State for the Environment by an official working party, one of the paragraphs contained this incredible conclusion: 'In effect, we are consciously and deliberately accumulating a toxic substance on the off-chance that it may be possible to get rid of it at a later date. We are committing future generations to tackle a problem which we do not know how to handle.'

Here is a classic case of a nihilistic society, although it must be emphasised some members deplore to belong to such a society. More than sixty years have elapsed since the intense argument developed, yet scientists can find no way of closing this Pandora's box. Suggestions have been considered in shooting the evil stuff into cosmic space or burying the stuff in the entrails of the earth, but such a policy, out of sight, out of mind is the absurdity of all absurdities. When man plays the part of God, he is unaware of the huge burden of responsibility that he undertakes. The vexing problem today is that most politicians have eliminated the word responsibility from their vocabulary. **Ralph and Mildred Buchsbaum** insisted, 'Ecology, indeed, ought to be a compulsory subject for all economists, whether professional or laymen, as this might serve to restore at least a modicum of balance.' One cannot argue with this statement except that ecology ought to be a compulsory subject for politicians as well.

In a debate on the 'Windscale Inquiry Report' which took place on the 22 March 1978, the Secretary of State for the Environment welcomed the debate, 'because I believe that the matters covered by the Windscale Report go far beyond those normally raised by a planning inquiry. On this occasion, I have chosen a different way. What is unique to this case is that the planning application itself, for outline planning permission to construct a major chemical engineering plant for reprocessing spent oxide nuclear fuel at Windscale, is patently of small importance compared with the major environmental, national and international issues.'

The different way was just another method to bulldoze through planning consent for the construction of the nuclear reprocessing plant, and it was a watershed in our industrial society whereby it opted for a plutonium economy. What was unique to the case was that the ecological, ethical and metaphysical arguments were dismissed, only the scientific and technological arguments were accepted. Fears were expressed that Britain would become the nuclear dustbin of the world which was seen by the government as big business which would assist our balance of payments. The disposal of the world's nuclear waste was a problem that was never considered in any great depth, otherwise the construction of nuclear power stations would not have been permitted until such information was available.

The Secretary for State pointed out, 'It has often been said that the proposal to process oxide nuclear fuel is inseparably linked to a major nuclear programme involving fast breeder reactors. As the inspector rightly concludes, the case for reprocessing can be judged on its merits, independently of the question whether we decide to embark upon a fast breeder programme.' This time, the 'logic of relations' was dismissed, as well as the question, what comes first, the chicken or the egg? The latter also relates to causation when a first thing is necessary for the occurrence of a second thing.

Procrastinating over the decision to embark upon a fast breeder programme, **prior** to the consideration of the planning application for reprocessing spent oxide nuclear fuel suggested the connivance of a *fait accompli* situation. Accepting the inspector's judgement for planning consent paved the way for the introduction of the fast breeder reactor. The sequence was inseparably linked as opponents of the application claimed and the existence of the FBR at Sizewell now confirms the case. Is it any wonder that few citizens have little confidence in the impartiality of public inquiries as often their outcome appears predetermined by the weight of economic argument?

The Secretary of State explained, 'In dealing with these problems in the context of the Windscale Report, we are in fact facing the essence of the dilemma which the use of nuclear power poses for mankind. The dilemma has been there from the start, and with it the key question of how the peaceful development of nuclear power can be promoted without radiation and harm to our own and succeeding generations and without at the same time opening up the threat of the ever-wider spread of nuclear weapons.'

From the very beginning of the argument, 'Ought man to split atoms?' it was asserted that a dilemma existed. Now a dilemma may be defined as a predicament giving the choice of evil actions. This was not true; no dilemma existed; it was solely a matter of choice. It was nonsense to relate the rejection of the development of nuclear power to an evil action, it was the converse. However, at the time of the Windscale Inquiry debate, a dilemma had emerged over the development of nuclear power and the choice was either to stop the evil action or continue the evil action, the stock-piling of plutonium waste. A professor at King's College London, **Jack Mahoney** suggested a maxim having a far greater impact than the one favoured by some local authorities which is far more comprehensive; *vis apud nos nuclearis arcenda*, (nuclear power must be banned from our midst).

Reflecting upon the threat of the proliferation of nuclear weapons, this ought to have been considered when scientists discovered the nature of atoms, nuclear reaction and the lethal by-products. If members of our government wish to stop the spread of nuclear weapons, then they ought to behave differently from the Scribes and the Pharisees, for the policy 'don't do as we do, do as we tell you,' is scornful. For over four decades, various politicians have sung the praises of nuclear deterrence as having prevented a third major European War. Most historians now affirm that Stalin had no plans to extend his borders beyond the territories annexed in 1945. The obsession with deterrence led to the stock-piling of strategic nuclear weapons, yet the madness was exposed by a former US president, 'A nuclear war cannot be won and should not be fought.' When a former prime minister was asked, 'When would you press the nuclear button?' the bluff was called. The theory of nuclear deterrence is nothing more than a nihilistic 'I dare you game,' whereby our participation in this nihilistic game prostitutes the values that we wish to defend. To participate in this nuclear game with weapons of terror and simultaneously to condemn acts of terrorism implicitly obeys the law of contradiction. Those human beings who believe there is ever justification for pressing the nuclear button forfeit their right to be called a human being; they are savages. Those human beings who believe there is never justification for pressing the nuclear button, yet still believe in keeping our nuclear deterrent, they are irrational. Those human beings who believe that nuclear weapons can serve no purpose in our defence policy and advocate unilateral nuclear disarmament, they win the moral and logical argument. In subscribing to a policy of unilateral nuclear disarmament, our representative at the United Nations could stand tall and lecture about the proliferation of nuclear weapons without any fear of being associated with the Scribes and Pharisees.

The problem of disposing of high-level radioactive waste also involves another enormous problem, what happens to the actual nuclear reactor housing when it is made redundant? It was known at the very beginning they could not be dropped like a tall chimney or taken apart in pieces, but that they were destined to remain in position for far longer than the whole of human history. In the fifties, the proponents of nuclear power were so blinkered by the short-term gains that they were blind to the fact, that in the long term, they had created Frankenstein monsters which are incomparable with any prehistoric monster. Once Pandora's atomic box was opened, the evils flew out to multiply, which is confirmed by the fact that over 400 nuclear reactors have been constructed world-wide. Another Pandora's box labelled **GMO** (Genetically Modified Organisms) exists on planet Earth. The habit of human stupidity persists.

Existing society treats consumption as the ultimate end of all economic activity. Why? Because consumption means that goods are sold and when goods are sold to any extent, then there is a strong possibility of making a profit. However, the goods must be delivered to the point of sale in quick time, so there is a premium upon speed, not only in the production of goods but also in their delivery. Now, speed may be defined as either the rate of increase in production or the rate of increase in distance with respect to the function of time. Hence, the function of time as well as money is important in a free market economy.

A previous government's 'Transport White Paper' with the persuasive title, 'Roads to Prosperity' was published at the end of 1989 and the document was full of bigotry. A more realistic title would have been 'Roads to Poverty,' for the £12 billion planned to be spent on road building would result in a poor environment, poor health and a poor quality of life.

In October 1994, the 'Royal Commission on Environmental Pollution' presented its report. The main recommendation in the report was that targets for increasing the use of public transport are essential and measures must be introduced to curb the growth of road freight and cars. The response by the transport minister, **Steven Norris** was, 'We all recognise that chasing car ownership is a pretty silly thing to do. For the sake of the environment, we must try to tone down this love affair with the car.' Credibility is tested as four years previously the Transport Department was encouraging a love affair with the car.

In April 1996, the report 'Blueprint 5: The True Cost of Road Transport' was published. The government funded the study and the research team was led by Professor **David Pearce,** an economist and former advisor to ministers at the Department of Environment. The significant conclusion in the report is that the true cost of road transport (the use of motor cars and lorries) amounts to the staggering total of £50 billion a year; this is double the amount estimated by the Royal Commission on Environmental Pollution. The costs relate to healthcare, damage to public buildings and lost production through lack of sleep by wage and salary workers. Traffic pollution accounts for 6,000 premature deaths per year which is double the road accidents. The report includes the assertion that 32 million people are exposed to noise pollution from traffic and such pollution increases the risk of heart disease, circulation disorders, depression and learning difficulties for children. Finally, the authors of the report insist that steps must be taken to reduce the risk to public health, damage to buildings and the threat of global warming.

It is a *schizophrenic* aspect of existing society that the consumer should not act in the same way as the producer, that is, to cut consumption costs to the minimum; this would be contrary to the economic calculus. If the consumers considered their costs with the same discipline as the producers and service businesses, then it would have a devastating effect upon the economy. The industrial system which had destroyed the rural economy by attracting agricultural workers to city jungles would become true jungles if anarchy reigned. This scenario can develop from the two consequences of ignoring the virtue *temperance*— (i) the ever-increasing size of debt taken on by citizens, businesses and governments, or living far in excess of income, and (ii) the ever-decreasing stocks of fossil fuels which governments treat as income, as if the production system can replace this natural capital.

The word 'economy' equates to a careful and judicious use of anything like time, money and energy. Time relates to money; time relates to energy stocks available; money relates to the cost of energy. Now, the careful and judicious use of energy means that we must plan our operations so that we reduce the amount of energy used which introduces the concept of 'motion economy.' In wartime Britain, the following question appeared on posters throughout the country—is your journey really necessary? Reason urges us to take notice of the poster once again. If we accept that at some future date, we will have to cut down on our journeys, then why not now? Procrastination is the thief of time, yet we continue to act without a care for posterity.

The Club of Rome was set up in 1968, which led to the publication of *The Limits to Growth*. The principal conclusion by the authors was that the *longer laissez faire* was accepted as the doctrine, then it was inevitable that there would be a global economic and environmental crisis of such magnitude, so as to make any human solution virtually impossible. In the same period, *A Blueprint for Survival* was drawn up with the help of eminent medical, scientific, economic and sociological specialists. The conclusion they deduced from the abundance of information was that the industrial society with its dogmatic belief in its *ethos of growth,* is not sustainable in the long term as Nature will not tolerate empire builders.

In June 1972, a conference was convened in Stockholm and some 1200 delegates and advisors attended to discuss the 'Human Environment.' In conjunction with the Stockholm conference, 'Friends of the Earth' published a book with the appropriate title, *Only One Earth.* In its appendix were the proposed principles of the Human Environment; the first principle remains valid yet to a large extent it has been ignored. 'Man has the fundamental right to adequate conditions of life, in an environment of a quality which permits a life of dignity and well-being, and bears a solemn responsibility to protect and enhance the environment for future generations.'

The title *Only One Earth* states an ontological fact, but this question must be answered, 'Why was man put on planet Earth?' **Dr Montefiore** knew the answer, 'Until men come to believe in their hearts that all life is held in trust from God, there can be no valid ethical reason why we should owe a duty to posterity. Once it is believed that men hold their dominion over all nature as stewards and trustees for God, then immediately they are confronted by an inalienable duty towards and concern for their total environment, present and future; and this duty towards environment does not merely include other human beings, but all nature and all life.'

Chapter 11
Philos Sophia

Philosophy is a subject that defies a satisfactory definition. 'What is philosophy?' poses a philosophical question. The word derived from the Greeks, literally means, 'love of wisdom,' therefore, a philosopher is a 'lover of wisdom.' However, it is not valid to presume that a philosopher is a wise man. At his trial, **Socrates** informed his accusers that the reason why he practised philosophy was that 'the unexamined life was not worth living...are you not ashamed of your eagerness to possess as much wealth, reputation and honours as possible, while you do not care for nor give thought to wisdom and truth, or the best condition of your soul?' It cannot be denied, a philosopher has acquired knowledge, but there is a distinction between wisdom and knowledge as will be made clear shortly.

Possibly, a metaphorical explanation may best prepare the ground: philosophy germinates in the soil of solitude from which the roots of reflection, speculation and analysis grow. Silence and steadfast attention are the stems for understanding as the bud of conscience thirsts for the flower of truth as to why different forms of life exist, and in this hierarchical structure, the perennial question arises—is there a divine being?

Pythagoras is usually associated with the discovery of a mathematical theorem. However, he thought that form or structure was the proper object of study. **Pythagoras** believed that just as the universe is *cosmos* or an orderly system, so all human beings are a *cosmos* or a miniature orderly system. In this miniature, *cosmos* is the soul which seeks purification, so that pure spirit is able to return to the universal spirit. By studying structure and form, it helps us to develop a character whereby form and order exist in ourselves, then we become *Cosmios* or the soul becomes an orderly system.

Having referred to the theorem of **Pythagoras**, it becomes manifest to the author that mathematics is a kind of bait that attracts a person to philosophy. In the simple equation, $y = 1 \div x$, we find that as y moves closer and closer to zero then x tends to 'infinity.' An alert student will inquire, 'Is infinity a number?' The answer is in the negative and x is never considered as zero. An infinite amount of time would be necessary to count an infinite number. An infinite amount of time equates to eternity, so what is time?

Inevitably, questions are raised concerning infinity. How can a finite mind conceive infinity? Is the universe finite or infinite? Which has the higher reality, the finite or the infinite? Is the infinite incomplete, or are finite objects the proof of a higher level of being?

By the use of a vector diagram which shows both magnitude and direction, we let j be an operator that rotates in an anti-clockwise direction. From certain equations, we determine that $j = \sqrt{-1}$. It is inferred that $x + jy$ can be plotted at the position whose co-ordinates are x and y. In this complex number, x is called the real part and jy the imaginary part.

The purpose of dwelling on the complex number is to reveal a contradiction that may puzzle a student. Earlier in the learning curve, a student grasps that $1 \times 1 = 1$ and $-1 \times -1 = 1$.

In the equation $x \times x = -1$, we know that -1 has no square root. Such a circumstance raises a pertinent question—what is truth in mathematics and how are its truths related to proofs? After a study of the 'unified theory of numbers,' a student is able to understand why **Bertrand Russell** was prompted to make this statement, 'mathematics may be defined as the subject in which we do not know what we are talking about nor whether what we are saying is true.' Mathematics can make no assertions about the universe or about man's relationship with it. Of course, mathematics gives us a high degree of certainty in specific areas and many claim that science and mathematics should guide philosophy. This is absurd! Both are very efficient at dealing with the dead aspect of nature; when they become involved with the origination of human life they are out of their depth, yet there has been an attempt to drown the faith of human beings by scientific jargon.

The value truth relates to sentences, statements, propositions as well as beliefs. Theories of truth can be reduced to two main divisions—one involving the acceptance of truth as a property of *representations* of some kind arising from language or mind; the other involving the acceptance of truth as a property of *propositions* arising from speech or thought.

The most common theory of truth is the *correspondence* theory which implicates a relation between two entities— (i) that which is true (a statement, a proposition or a belief) and (ii) that which provides the proof it is true (a fact, an event, or an existing situation), in a single word, it 'corresponds.' This theory has been recognised as circular since a fact is only made plain via truth.

The *correspondence* theory appeals to those who separate the knower from the known. Idealists reject this theory; they prefer the *coherence* theory. The concept implies that anything is true if it coheres, or it is logically consistent with a larger system of belief. Obviously, such a theory tends to *relativism,* and critics argue that there is a muddle between proposing a criterion of truth and asserting what truth comprises.

Pragmatists, especially politicians, accept that truth has no practical value and whether our beliefs are true or false does not matter; all that matters is our happiness and well-being. The Sophists had adopted a similar attitude when arguing with **Socrates**. Pragmatism appears to work only in the short-term.

Truth cannot be isolated from belief, also knowledge and belief are interrelated, further, belief implicates concept. A belief appertains to mind and involves the conclusion that a proposition, a statement or a fact is either true or false. However, the analysis of belief is a study of its relations with dispositions, actions and also internal and external experiences.

Certainly, 'belief in' equates to a creed which is a system of religious belief. There are those who claim that 'belief-in' God is no different to 'belief-in' Father Christmas, therefore it is necessary to justify the belief. Religion involves the concept of *revelation* which means a direct communication between God and man. It is not suggested that such a revelation is impossible but it is a revelation to only the first person. When the recipient of the revelation informs another person, it is a communication between man and man, therefore, revelation is restricted to the first communication as the further communication is only a report.

From this criticism, a reader may be inclined to assume the author is an agnostic. However, besides a particular revelation, there is a universal revelation; the word of God is implicit in the solar system in which different kinds of being exist; there is a hierarchic structure implicating the movement from the inanimate to the animate and the progression from one to another adds a further property;

that is, matter, life, consciousness and self-knowledge. This is sufficient reason for the author to believe that a divine plan is in operation and there is an amazing designer existing somewhere in the universe.

The evolutionary theory emerging from Darwin's *Origin of Species* is based on 'chance' and 'natural selection,' thus it indicates that it lacks a *teleological* factor. It gives no account of the development of human society and its culture. Anyone who disputes that a divine being exists must consider this fact—no person can prove that God does not exist. Is it conceivable that from mere 'chance,' such a logical impossibility was derived?

Today, most human beings are influenced by science, including physics rather than by metaphysics. They do not understand that science has strict limitations. In the last century, the pursuers of science insisted that human life had no meaning or purpose having emerged by 'chance.' Present day scientists now insist that they deal with specific, strictly isolated systems and how they function. Such systems can give us no guidance on the meaning and purpose of human life. It is strange the way Darwin's Theory now looks fragile; physicists have discovered a mysterious mathematical order in the sub-atomic physical world. This has motivated some to dissociate themselves from their predecessors' materialistic scientism; their minds have been opened to admit transcendent reality.

Reality relates to existence, although some philosophers have argued that there are only appearances. Nevertheless, in 'The Second Coming,' **WB Yeats** transmits a vision that cannot be dismissed, for there is abundant evidence to confirm that western civilisation is fast approaching a dangerous point.

Things fall apart, the centre cannot hold;
Mere anarchy is loosed upon the world.

The centre holds the store of knowledge from which we acquire our profound convictions. Two subjects are locked in this centre store, that is, metaphysics and ethics. Criticism of meta physics propounded by sceptical philosophers led to the call to abandon metaphysics, but how is it possible to abandon being or levels of being? As the attitude exists, then it is justifiable to conclude that this is stupid metaphysics.

There is no subject in greater confusion than ethics. Moral philosophers tended to pursue an investigation without first explaining the purpose of human life. The polar concepts, good and evil, right and wrong are inextricably linked to purpose. What is the purpose of being good? What is the purpose of making sure an action is right?

In his *Principia Ethica,* **GE Moore** maintained that to seek the purpose or suggest what is good, can always be countered by the response. 'But is that good?' The 'Good' cannot be defined or analysed according to **Moore** which he called the 'naturalistic fallacy.' The philosopher would have made a good politician for this is a classic case of evasion. **Bishop Gore** argued, 'No man wishes to be good without feeling also that vice is ugly and is out of harmony with the truth.'

Jesus Christ said, 'If ye apply my teaching...Then ye will know the truth, and the truth will set ye free.' (John 8:31–32). Society has attempted to ignore the words of this great religious leader; it has conducted an experiment by allowing most of its members to live without any creed. The experiment has failed. Why? Because moral problems cannot be solved by scientific method.

The limitations of science have caused many to despair or to escape from the social problems. Human beings need help; previously they thought they could conquer nature, but nature was just giving them more rope. By providence, the Christian church has been given a unique opportunity to revise its creed, to make it credible and consistent. Such action would attract liberal thinkers from varied backgrounds who would support the church in its rational revision. Unjustifiably, the Reverend **David Jenkins** was accused of being a 'muddled man,' yet he was acutely aware that some statements in the Bible were beyond belief.

There are three main branches of philosophy—speculative, practical and critical. The latter philosophy is embodied in the principle of the Frankfurt School, namely, all biased doctrines must come under the microscope of criticism, and science cannot remain value-free, thus avoiding value judgements. So, this principle justifies criticism of the Bible, although the author of 'Revelations' warned that anyone who interferes with this book must suffer pestilence. Is it possible for a God of Love to be simultaneously a God of Vengeance?

It has been asserted that the Bible is a very good servant but an extremely bad master. Many erudite writers have described the Bible as a book of history and theology besides a literary work. Coincidently, the Bible is three books in one—it is a book of mythology, a book of mysticism and a book of wisdom. Here is an apt example, 'The things that are unseen are far more significant than the things that are seen, for the things that are seen are temporal, whereas the things that are unseen are eternal.' (2 Corinthians 4:18).

With regard to certain historical events, it has been suggested that the Bible should be interpreted symbolically rather than literally. This may be appropriate for some events in the Old Testament, but the narrative account of persons and events in the New Testament must come under closer scrutiny, because it contains religious teachings that are the foundation for a universal religion. Scripture ratifies that Jesus Christ had also sinned. Responding to an inquiry from a rich man, Jesus said, 'Why do you call me good? None are good except one, that is God.' (Luke 18:19). Via self-knowledge, Jesus confessed that he was not good, so how could he have been God-incarnate? Is it possible to conceive that God-incarnate would sin? God would be just like a mortal man, prone to wrongdoing.

Again, when referring to Scripture, Paul confirmed the statement made by Jesus in his letter to the Romans, 'All have sinned and fall short of the glory of God.' (Romans 3:23). He reached this conclusion via self-knowledge as another letter to the Romans confirms—my own behaviour troubles me. For that which I wish to do I refuse to do, yet I do what I really hate. If I do what I do not wish to do…it is no longer I who do it—it must be sin that dwell in my nature. (Romans 7:15–17). So, we are drawn to this valid conclusion—all men are born to be sinners, but by the recognition of this fact, they can struggle to become free from sin or moral wrongdoing; this is the struggle for perfect freedom.

Must religion always be a chord of dischord? Any universal ideal must be based upon some substantive belief before any unity of civilisation is possible. The Lord Buddha advised, 'Do not have blind faith. Accept as truth that which after a thorough investigation, and according to your experience agrees with your reason.' **Clifford Hill** wrote, 'There are thousands of ministers in all the major denominations today who have been brought up in the tradition of liberal Biblical theology, who have sincere and honest doubts about the most basic tenets of Christian doctrine. I spent a few hours recently with a bishop in the Church of England who doesn't believe in the Resurrection. It is not unknown even for the principal of a theological college to deny the divinity of Jesus Christ. I often speak to ministers who admit that they have no faith and don't know what they really believe.'(They are role-acting only.)

The three basic tenets of Christian doctrine at the centre of constant controversy, are the virgin birth, the resurrection and the divinity of Jesus Christ.

The failure of the churches can be traced to two main factors (i) The weak theological interpretation of the Scriptures. (ii) The material and political aspirations of the Roman Catholic, Greek Orthodox and Protestant Churches. Church history has led to division between the evangelicals and social action Christians; the obstinacy of the evangelicals is conceding ground to the march of secular forces.

The evangelicals have no influence to awaken society to the dangers of political and economic forces that are responsible for the degeneration of society. The 'Protestant Reformation' was a petty revolt; the time, 2000 years after the birth of a great religious leader is perfect for a 'Revisionist Movement' to prevent a further disintegration of the Christian Church. First, **John Donne's** metaphor ought to be persistently proclaimed, paraphrased as follows—no human being is an island existing alone; every human being is a piece of the planet, a part of the universe. Second, the Christian Creeds ought to be subjected to a radical revision. And third, the main activity of the Church must be centred on the teachings of Jesus Christ, not the way he entered and departed from this world. Constant attention should be focused on the rebuke he made in his political speech to the crowd in Jerusalem. (Matthew 23).

Jesus showed abundant sympathy for the poor and the frail in society; he was deeply concerned about social justice and he was critical of social privilege. Jesus argued that social justice relates to the belief that all human beings are treated equally by God as each has an equal share of God's love. Jesus thought that God's love is a reason for reciprocity, so he composed the two unique commandments. The first commandment—Thou shalt love God with the utmost sincerity. The second is like it: Thou shalt love thy neighbour as thyself. (Matthew 22:37–39).

The church doctors acted like King Lear; they wanted it both ways. They insisted on Scripture being their sole guide, yet they accepted the pagan doctrine of *justum bellum* (just war). They disregarded Jesus, 'Love your enemies, bless them that curse you, do good to them that hate you, and pray for them which despitefully use you, and persecute you.' (Matthew 5:43–44). Accepting that Jesus said, 'Love your enemies,' then if any religion rejects his pacifist doctrine, it is a pseudo-religion. A contradiction is a conjunction of a proposition and its negation—love your enemies and do not love your enemies.

Some critics have complained that the principles of Jesus Christ are too strong for human beings to hold. This is chiefly due to the general misunderstanding about the use of the word 'love.' Many persons associate the word 'love' with emotion or passion and the physical relationship between a man and a woman, The Greek meaning of 'love' is not related to any kind of emotion; it is a deliberate disposition of the will; it is within every person's power to possess providing it is recognised. To love thyself is to recognise that the gift of life (which so in any do not value) is abundant wealth and it ought to be used for good ends.

After Jesus had informed a lawyer of the two great commandments, the lawyer challenged Jesus, 'And who is my neighbour?' In reply, Jesus recounted the action of the *Good Samaritan* (Luke 10:30–37) which teaches that you do not ignore the plight of a human being, and your neighbour is any human being who needs help. In existing society, there is the absurd phenomenon of many neighbours who are strangers. It appears that it is only in times of adversity like war or a huge natural disaster that man realises he is a social being. One of the chief reasons why society is in general decline is that individualism and competition have been fostered to the utmost degree.

How can I love or help my neighbour if I cannot love or help myself? That is, when I am critical of my own behaviour in discovering that I am not good but inclined to sin. To be able to love or help my neighbour, I must first love God. This is attained by striving to direct the mind on things of perfection that are above my own level of being; this is the realm of the sovereign good.

In his excellent book, 'To Have or To Be,' **Erich Fromm** analysed the two modes of existence that human beings have the option to make:(i) The 'having' mode which is dominated by material possessions and consumption, thus fostering greed, envy and aggressiveness. (ii) The 'being' mode which is embodied in shared experiences, consideration, co-operation leading to rational productivity rather than futile activity; its source is love embracing the belief that spiritual values precede material values.

Many persons enter into politics because they wish to help to create a better society. **Erich Fromm** perceived that they wish to change and improve the character of society but they soon become disillusioned. Why? **Erich Fromm** argued that it is impossible to change the character of society until the character of the individual is changed. **Socrates** realised this and his statement showed his exasperation, 'The curse of ignorance is that a man who is neither good nor wise remains self-satisfied; he lacks the will to acquire that of which he feels no want.' Of course, **Socrates** believed that the pursuit of virtue is important in the process

189

of character building. Character is expressed in behaviour, influenced and inspired by principle, self-knowledge and practical wisdom. In its sublime form, it is the individual soul guided by reason, religion and morality. In the affairs of human life, it is not intelligence that is the foundation of character, it is self-control, patience and discipline aided by sound judgement. Self-control is **a key** factor in the formation of character and it is the precondition for all the virtues; it is the principal distinction between an animal and a human being.

Herbert Spencer wrote, 'The supremacy of self-control consists of one of the perfections of man. Not to be impulsive, not to be spurred hither and thither by each desire that in turn comes uppermost, but to be self-restrained, self-balanced, governed by the joint decision of the feelings in counsel assembled, before whom every action shall have been debated and calmly determined—it is that which education, moral education at least, strives to produce.'

Augustine thought that the very perfection of man is to discover his own imperfections. The inclination to sin indicates an imperfection in character. Today, the younger generation is not influenced by traditional wisdom but only by science, so few know the difference between science and wisdom. **Augustine** discerned that science performs two roles: (i) science for exploitation; (ii) science for comprehension which equates to wisdom. Alas! In the *Inferno,* that is, the existing world of sin and corruption, power and wealth are treated as ends rather than as means, and wisdom has been made a subordinate of science, if not made redundant.

Etienne Gilson explained in 'The Christian Philosophy of St Augustine' the difference between science and wisdom: 'The real difference which set the one against the other derives from the nature of their objects. The object of wisdom is such that, by reason of its intelligibility alone, no evil use can be made of it; the object of science is such that it is in constant danger of falling into the clutches of cupidity (greed of gain), owing to its very materiality. Hence, the double designation we may give science according as it is subservient to appetite, as it is whenever it chooses itself as an end, or is subservient to wisdom, as it is whenever it is directed to the sovereign good.'

Besides the lack of self-control, many members of society lack faith and discipline. The lack of discipline relates to lack of obedience, or a refusal to obey the rules, especially on the roads. Discipline is not a burden when good habits become a routine. One of the best habits that can be performed is to repeat a prayer several times each day, which is a means to self-knowledge. *Dear God, forgive me for my sinful nature, have mercy upon me, for I repent and shall strive to sin no more*. The daily repetition of this short prayer induces a spiritual current that refines and reforms the individual's character. It is open to every sceptic to test, but perhaps this is expecting too much as the sceptic lacks the will to believe.

Great moral leaders have been exceptional individuals and greatness is but relative. The destiny of most individuals in life is so limited, however, each individual can act his/her role to the best of his/her ability; in other words, each can do his/her duty. It has been pointed out that the Tory Party represents the Church of England, and also, socialism owes more to Methodism than Marxism. The main proposals for the supposed improvement in society are contained in the manifestos of political parties. When politicians argue that church leaders ought not to interfere in the affairs of politics and they should concentrate on theological matters, then the reaction of **Bishop Berkeley** is justified, 'He who hath not meditated upon God, the human mind and the *summum bonum* may make a thriving earthworm but a sorry statesman.'

It would be an act of prejudice to exclude the three theological values, namely, faith, hope and love. First, some dismiss faith and rely solely on reason, but **Immanuel Kant** spotted the error, 'There is a limit where the intellect fails and breaks down, and this limit is where the questions concerning God, freewill and immortality arise.' To have no faith in God is to have no rational purpose of life. Faith without right action is also to have no purpose. Scripture criticises, 'Faith by itself, if not supplemented by action is dead…You, foolish man…faith without works is useless…You see then how by works a man is justified, and not by faith alone.'

One of the biological needs which we tend to neglect is our need for love and companionship; the modern lifestyle, broken marriages, single-parent families, love starved children, the lack of a code of ethics, all are contributing to the increase in health problems. Good relationships depend upon quality and commitment, and love grows by 'treating others as you would like them to treat you.' The predicament of society is that there is a deficiency of love; there is a lack of love for God; there is a lack of love for neighbour, or allowing time to be spent in communication, consideration, aid and sympathy.

It has been often questioned, 'Why does God permit evil to exist?' **Augustine** argued, 'Either God cannot abolish evil or God will not; if God cannot abolish evil, then God is not omnipotent; if God will not abolish evil, then God is not benevolent.' **Augustine** asserted that why things are as they are is beyond human understanding, for if it is accepted that God is good, then God cannot desire what is evil. The problem of evil was not a problem for the theologian **Friedrich von Hugel** who emphasised—the greater our intensity of belief in God, the greater our repulsion of evil, and the greater our compassion for those who suffer from adversity.

In his 'Essay on Man,' **Alexander Pope** insisted, 'Hope springs eternal in the human breast.' In **Bertrand Russell's** autobiography, there is a profound passage of emotion which revealed his philanthropy:

I may have thought the road to a world of free and happy human beings shorter than it is proving to be, but I was not wrong in thinking that such a world is possible, and it is worth living with a view to bringing it nearer. I have lived in pursuit of a vision, both personal and social. Personal: to care for what is noble, for what is beautiful, for what is gentle; to allow moments of insight to give wisdom at more mundane times. Social: to see in imagination the society that is to be created, where individuals grow freely, and where hate and greed and envy die because there is nothing left to nourish them. These things, I believe, and the world, for all its horrors has left me unshaken.

The message is unmistakable, *nil desperandum*; remember—the greatest power that a human being can have is the power of character; the greatest wealth that a human being can have is a true sense of values, which implicates truth, beauty and goodness, emanating from the character of GOD.

Bibliography

Bantock, G. H. (1965) *Education and Values,* Faber.

Behnke, H., Bachmann, F., Fladt, F., and Suss, W. (1974) *Fundamentals of Mathematics* trans by Gould,S. H., MIT.

Berger Peter, L. (1976) *Invitation to Sociology*, Penguin.

Blackham, H. J. (1952) *Six Existentialist Thinkers,* Routledge and Kegan Paul.

Blackmore, Richard and Hughes John (1714) *The lay Monastery,* Ferdinando Burleigh.

Blofeld John (1979) *Taoism,* Unwin.

Bradley, F. H. (1951) *Appearance and Reality,* OUP.

Cahn Steven, **M.** (ed.) (1990) *Classics of Western Philosophy,* Hackett.

Callow, Rev. C. A. (1899) *A History of the Creeds,* Elliot Stock.

Copi Irving (1961) *Introduction to logic,* Collier-Macmillan.

Cornford, F. M. (1932) *Before and After Socrates,* CUP.

Cornford, F. M. (1935) *Plato's Theory of Knowledge,* Kegan Paul.

Cornford, F. M. (1941) *Plato's Republic*, OUP.

Cornford, F. M. (1950) *The Unwritten Philosophy*, CUP.

Cosmo Umberto (1950) *A handbook, lo Dante Studies* trans. by David Moore, Blackwell.

Dakin, A. H. (1934) *Von Hugel and the Supernatural,* Macmillan.

Davies Paul (1983) *God and New Physics,* Dent.

Durkin, H. E. (1937) *An Experimental Study of Problem Solving,* Archives of Psychology, New York.

Erdmann Johann Eduard (1890) *A history of Philosophy, Ancient and Mediaeval,* Allen & Unwin.

Ewing, A. C. (1963) *Ethics*, EUP.

Finnis, J. (1980) *Natural law and Natural Rights,* OUP.

Friends of the Earth (1972) *The Stockholm Conference; Only, One Earth,* Earth Island.

Galbraith John Kenneth (1985) *The Affluent Society,* Andre Deutsch.

Gasset Jose Ortegay (1961) *The Modern Theme,* Harper and Row.

Gewirth, A. (1980) *Reasoning and Morality,* VOC.

Gilson Etienne (1928) *The Unity of Philosophical Experience,* Sheed and Ward.

Gilson Etienne (1956) *The Christian Philosophy of St Thomas Aquinas,* Hutchinson.

Gilson Etienne (1960) *The Christian Philosophy of St Augustine,* Hutchinson.

Gore Charles (1935) *The Philosophy of the Good Life,* Dent.

Gosling, J.C. B. (1969) *Pleasure and Desire,* OUP.

Griffin, J. (1986) *Well-being,* OUP.

Guthrie, **W. K.** C. (1950) *The Greek Philosophers from Thales to Aristotle,* Methuen.

Hardy, G. H. and Wright E.M. (1979) *An Introduction to the Theory of Numbers,* OUP.

Harer, M. (1952) *The Language of Morals,* OUP.

Harer, M. (1963) *Freedom and Reason,* OUP.

Harer, M. (1981) *Moral Thinking,* OUP.

Harrison Sidney (1947) *Music for the Multitude*, Michael Joseph.

Hill Clifford (1980) *Towards The Dawn*, Fount.

Hill, C. P. (1977) *British Economic and Social History, 1700–1975*, Arnold.

Hospers John (1956) *An Introduction to Philosophical Analysis*, Routledge and Kegan Paul.

Jaspers Karl (1956) *Reason and Existence*, Routledge and Kegan Paul.

Jennings **William** trans. (1895) *The Confucian Analects*, Routledge.

Jeans James (1930) *The Mysterious Universe*, CUP.

Kelly, J. N. D. (1960) *Early Christian Creeds*, Longman.

Keynes, J. M. (1931) *Economic Possibilities for our Grandchildren, Essays in Persuasion*, Macmillan.

Keynes, J. M. (1973) *The General Theory of Employment, Interest and Money*, Macmillan.

King George V, *Speech extracted from The Times* 12.4.19.

King James, *Holy Bible 1611*, Eyre and Spottiswoode.

Lewis, C. S. (1978) *The Abolition of Man*, Fount.

Lovejoy, A.O. (1960) *The Great Chain of Being*, Harper & Row.

Meade James (1964) *Efficiency, Equality and the Ownership of Capital*, Allen and Unwin.

Meadows, D. (1972) *The Limits to Growth*, MIT.

Montefiore, H. (1969) *The Question Mark*, Collins.

Moore, G. E. (1960) *Principia Ethica*, CUP.

Nozick, R. (1974) *Anarchy, State and Utopia*, Blackwell.

Parsons Talcott (1952) *The Social System*, Tavistock.

Pascal Blaise (1966) *Pensees*, Penguin.

Pieper Joseph (1960) *Prudence* trans. by Richard and Clara Winston, Faber.

Plato (1980) *The Symposium* trans. by Walter Hamilton, Penguin.

Pope Alexander (1963) *The Poems of Alexander Pope,* ed. John Butt, **New** Haven.

Popper Karl (1966) *The Open Society and Its Enemies*, Routledge and Kegan Paul.

Quick, O. C. (1938) *Doctrines of the Creed*, Nisbet.

Raphael, D. D. (1970) *Problems of Political Philosophy*, Pall Mall.

Rawls, J. (1972) *A Theory of Justice*, OUP.

Redmond, P. W. D. (1974) *General Principles of English Law*, Macdonald and Evans.

Robinson Joan (1966) *Economics, An Awkward Corner*, Allen and Unwin.

Robinson Joan (1970) *Freedom and Necessity*, Allen & Unwin.

Russell Bertrand (1946) *A History of Western Philosophy*, Allen & Unwin. Ryle Gilbert (1954) *Dilemmas*, CUP.

Ryle Gilbert (1967) *Tile Concept of Mind*, Hutchinson.

Sartre Jean Paul (1957) *Being and Nothingness*, Menthuen.

Sayers Dorothy, L. (1954) *Introductory Papers on Dante*, Menthuen.

Sayers Dorothy, L. and Reynolds Barbara (1962) *Dante-The Divine Comedy Ill; Paradise*, Penguin.

Schumacher, E. F. (1974) *Small is Beautiful*, Abacus.

Smith Adam (1970) *The Wealth of Nations*, Penguin.

Smith David (1987) *The Rise and Fall of Monetarism,* Penguin.

Stafford, L. W. T. (1976) *The Modern Economy*, Longman.

Stebbing, L. S. (1937) *Philosophy and the Physicist*, Methuen.

Stebbing, L. (1961) *SA Modern Introduction to Logic*, Methuen.

Swinburne, R (1979) *The Existence of God*, OUP.

Swinburne Richard (1981) *Faith and Reason*, OUP.

Tawney, R. H. (1921) *The Acquisitive Society*, Bell.

Thompson, J.B (1984) *Studies in the Theory of Ideology*, Polity.

Titmuss, R. M. **(1962)** *Income, Distribution and Social Change*, Allen and Unwin.

Tomlin, E.W. F. (1950) *The Western Philosophers*, Hutchinson.

Trilling Lionel (1967) *Beyond Culture*, Penguin.

Veblen Thorstein (1904) *The Theory of Business Enterprise*, Scribner.

Vernon, M. D. (1969) *Human Motivation*, CUP.

Waley, A. trans. (1938) *The Analects of Confucius*, Allen and Unwin.

Watson Jack B (1979) *Success in Twentieth Century Affairs,* John Murray.

Weber Max (1931) *The Protestant Ethic and the Spirit of Capitalism* trans. T. Parsons, Allen and Unwin.

Whitehead Alfred North (1933) *Adventures of Ideas*, CUP.

Wiggins David (1969) *Needs, Values Truth*, CUP.

Wilder-Smith, A. Ernest, (1975) G*od: To be or Not to be*, Telos.

Wilson John (1966) *Equality*, Hutchinson.

Wittgenstein, L. J. J. (1949) *Tractatus Logico-Philosophicus*, Routledge, Kegan and Paul.

Wittgenstein, L. J. J. (1965) *Philosophical Investigations*, Blackwell.

Yates, A. B(1962) *Frustration and Conflict*, Menthuen.

Abbreviations

CUP=Cambridge University Press
OUP=Oxford University Press
EUP=English Universities Press
MIT=Massachusetts Institute of Technology
UOC=University of Chicago

Where is the wisdom we have lost in knowledge? Where is the knowledge we have lost in information?

TS Eliot